AF718222

AN ANALYSIS OF RIGHTS

This book attempts to clarify a concept as common as it is mystifying even today. Discussions of right have not been wanting, yet surprisingly little has been done to analyse the concept in its full range. Moral and legal philosophers often advance divergent views – some describing a right as a claim, others as an entitlement, some putting the emphasis on interest, some on liberty, others on duty, and so on. The first four chapters deal specifically with these conceptual matters, as do also Chapters 5 and 6, the former a critique of Hohfeld's well-known schemata of rights, the latter an examination of such other 'right-like' notions as permission, power and privilege.

The next four chapters turn to the 'natural' foundations, or necessary discursive framework, of rights. Chapter 7 mainly tries to show that rights *qua* rights require a moral content of a certain kind, as a matter virtually of logical necessity, given the fact that we engage in moral argument to settle our interpersonal grievances, that is, argument which cannot take place except in terms of our mutual freedom and equality so long as we live as individuals amongst individuals, as members of the same community. Chapter 8 further considers three utterly basic rights, those of life, limb and property, while Chapter 9 discusses the question whether poverty can give rise to a natural right to welfare, and, if so, to what extent. The final chapter deals with the rights of someone – or something – not a normal adult; it offers a revised justification of children's rights, but opposes the idea of animals' rights without denying that animals, too, can have an interest against cruelty.

Samuel Stoljar is Professor of Law at the Research School of Social Sciences, the Australian National University, Canberra. A law graduate of the University of London, he has taught and lectured at many universities, most recently as Visiting Professor at the Universities of Paris I and II. He is a barrister-at-law of Gray's Inn, London, and a fellow of the Academy of Social Sciences of Australia.

His publications include *Moral and Legal Reasoning*.

K
760
S76
984
LAW LIBRARY
GOLDEN GATE UNIVERSITY

AN ANALYSIS OF RIGHTS

Samuel Stoljar

MACMILLAN

© S. J. Stoljar 1984

All rights reserved. No part of this publication may be reproduced or transmitted, in any form or by any means, without permission

First published 1984 by
THE MACMILLAN PRESS LTD
London and Basingstoke
Companies and representatives
throughout the world

Printed in Hong Kong

British Library Cataloguing in Publication Data
Stoljar, Samuel
An analysis of rights.
1. Rights (philosophy)
I. title
323.4'01 JC571
ISBN 0-333-37158-5

To N., J., D. and L

Contents

Preface ix

1 Rights, Claims and Entitlements **1**
Claims and Claiming 1
Making Claims and Having Rights 4
Claims and Entitlements 6
Subjunctive Claims 10

2 Rights as Defences and Liberties **13**
Defensive Rights: Their General Character 13
Rights and Liberties 15
Liberties: Other Versions 18
A Revised Dichotomy of Rights 22

3 Rights, Benefits and Interests **25**
Benefits and Interests 25
The Benefit-Theory: Objections I 27
The Benefit-Theory: Objections II 28
Interests and Rights 31
The Interest-Theory: A Postscript 34

4 Rights and Duties **36**
The Problem of Correlativity 36
Non-Correlative Duties 38
Non-Correlative Rights 40
Degrees of Correlativity 44
Correlatives and Complementaries 46
Right-Generality and Duty-Specificity 47

5 A Hohfeldian Digression **51**
Hohfeld's Basic Scheme 51
Rights, Liberties and No-Rights 53
The Duty–Liberty Relation 56

Power and Liability 58
Immunity and Disability 61

6 **Permission, Power and Privilege** **63**
Other Rights: Permissions 63
The Notion of Power 65
The Nature of Privilege 68
Derivative and Unequal Rights 71

7 **From Positive to Natural Rights** **74**
The Positive–Natural Distinction 74
Towards Natural Rights 77
Some Doctrines of Natural Rights 79
Equality and Freedom 81
A Rational Basis of Rights 84
Natural Rights and Moral Argument 87

8 **Life, Limb and Property** **90**
Inalienable and Alienable Rights 90
Public Natural Rights 93
Basic Rights and their Moral Direction 95
Conflict Among Basic Rights 97
The Right of Property I 100
The Right of Property II 102

9 **Rights to Welfare and Other Benefits** **105**
Welfare Rights: First Steps 105
Rights Against Community 108
The Quantum of Welfare 112
Rights to Other Benefits 115

10 **The Limits of Rights** **117**
Children's Rights 117
Concerning Other Rightholders 120
The Alleged Rights of Animals 122
Interest, Claims, Community: Final Remarks 124

Notes and References 126

Index 135

Preface

The following pages pursue problems briefly adverted to in a previous book but now receiving more probing and systematic study. My first great problem has been to identify the conceptual ingredients of a right: my second to explain the conditions under which an individual can, strictly, claim a natural right, irrespectively of actual laws or customs. These problems have made me follow different paths from those traced in two major, relatively recent contributions. While I, too, take rights seriously, I am here more interested in the concept of rights as distinct from a 'rights-thesis' such as propounded by Professor Dworkin. And while I, too, support certain forms of natural rights, I do so from premises emphatically narrower than those acceptable to Dr Finnis. Otherwise I have tried to take full account of the more than abundant literature, some of it legal, but mostly now in the philosophical journals; for I found my task to be one of having to argue my way through a large diversity of views in an effort to obtain at least some clearer perspectives.

SAMUEL STOLJAR

1 Rights, Claims and Entitlements

CLAIMS AND CLAIMING

What is a right? What is it to have one? Is it a claim, or an entitlement, or a liberty? Must it always relate to an interest or go with a correlative duty? Are there as well as positive or established also natural or moral rights, and, if so, of what sort and upon what sort of basis? To ask these – and, as we go on, other – questions is to reveal right as a very complex notion, with multiple aspects and elements, each inviting particular scrutiny.

Unlike a complicated object like a watch which is analysable according to whether, or how, its pieces fit into a unique structure, the components of a concept like right do not obey the same testable drill. A normative word, right is also relational – what logicians sometimes describe as a triadic relation – since in addition to the question as to who a right is for, there are two further questions as to who a right is to be against and what a right is to or about, with the further consequence that in different relational contexts different conceptual elements of right come to the fore. One element, however, plays a more primordial and persistent role, being also the element around which other threads can draw together; indeed if they did not, right would not form anything near a coherent concept but would be little more than a nominal facade screening disparate ideas. This connective component is that of 'claim' or 'claiming'. Many a dictionary entry in fact describes rights in terms of claims, and many treat claims as forms of right. Circular as they are, these definitions nevertheless call attention to a special link between rights and claims, the nature of which is still not as clear as it might be.

By claiming or making a claim we mean a speech-act, briefly that of demanding or calling for the return or recognition of something, but a verbal act normally made with some justificatory or supporting reason. To claim something is therefore not merely to demand it, it is more significantly to justify that demand with legitimate or legitimising grounds as to why the claimant should have it, why it is due to him, and so on. What these reasons are is not presently important; the point is that claiming is not just to clamour in a loud or insistent voice, not just to vociferate however imperatively. A robber, accordingly, can only demand rather than claim your money, but a scientific or intellectual argument cannot just demand acceptance, it can only claim to enunciate a truth at least worthy of consideration. In this way claiming plays a dual part which can be described as 'propositional' on the one hand and 'performative' on the other.[1] Propositionally, I may claim that such and such is or can be the case, or that I am entitled to a certain right, it being a feature of such claims that they are testable as to their truth, having regard either to the empirical evidence or, in the case of rights, to the source or rule or principle the right is said to be derived from. A performative claim rather puts the emphasis on what the right-holder does, namely, asking or calling for or demanding the return of what already belongs to him (his money, his book), or what should belong to him under given rules, such as where he applies for a patent or an old age pension, assuming he has met all eligible requirements. A propositional claim can then be more or less plausible, or stronger or weaker, according to our available knowledge or evidence, whereas performative claims do not vary in degree: one can, admittedly, make one's claim more or less strongly, but the right that is being claimed cannot similarly vary: to claim a right is thus virtually to exercise it, or, perhaps better, to take necessary steps towards exercising it.

This propositional–performative distinction, though it valuably identifies two separable meanings of the word 'claim', must not make us overlook that these two meanings often coalesce in practice. Where we claim what already belongs to us (our money, our purse), other words are equally capable of doing the same performative job; instead of claim we can use demand, ask, give, request, and so on. In saying, for example, 'Give me back my purse!', you both ask it back and give a sufficient reason for so asking (namely, that the purse is yours), without there being any particular need for the word 'claim'. Only where this justification is not clear does 'claim' come into its own, but then the performative sense of claiming merges with a strong propositional meaning. So when you say 'I claim this money' you say or imply that you want it back for a precise reason: that you have a right to it (it being your money), or that you represent somebody who has such a right (it being, for example, your child's money). It follows that to make a (valid) claim, i.e. a claim not manifestly false or fraudulent, is to imply that one already has, or has qualified for, a right to some *res* or benefit. Of course one can make a false claim, but even then one still pretends (falsely admittedly, but still pretends) to have a claim of some validity. Thus using the word 'claim', in 'I claim this money', instead of words like 'demand' or 'request' (the former a more brutal, the latter a more polite performative) is an implicit insistence on a right: as well as voicing a performative the creditor also issues a proposition that the money is truly his.

This result may appear to produce an oddity. If claiming already implies a right, a right one already has or is eligible to, does it not become strange to speak of claiming rights – almost as odd as it would be to speak of claiming claims? The oddity is however innocuous. For in claiming a right, the word 'claim' functions as a mere performative, a duplicate for 'demand' and so on, with the propositional role now becoming more silent or subdued. So used, moreover, the connection between claim and right may appear no more significant than that between right and any other performative. But this would be a wrong impression. For one thing, you cannot make a claim without having one, or at least stating to have something of a claim, which is precisely the difference between claiming and other performatives. For another, to demand a right implies having a (or some) claim to that right, since demanding a right is quite different from other demands such as demanding your money or your life.

This brings us to an even deeper connection between rights and claiming. You cannot *have* a right unless it can be claimed or demanded or insisted upon, indeed claimed effectively or enforceably. Two instances are often cited in which it looks as though one may have a right without making a claim. A person may be left a legacy without knowing anything about it, while children (they in particular) can have rights they are often not only ignorant of but also incapable of enforcing. Or, secondly, a person may be fully aware of having a right yet announce he is not going to claim it. In neither case, nevertheless, should we too hastily infer a radical disassociation of rights from claiming. For to have a right either means having a claim which has already been validly made or which is still validly makeable, so that to have a right, even if it does not imply actually making a claim, does imply having something claimable. Again, have a right must presuppose a claim *in limine*, namely, that a claim can be made to activate or establish that right, simply because rights are not self-executive but lie embedded in normative relationships. Rights thus are performative-dependent, their operative reality being their claimability; a right one could not claim, demand, ask to enjoy or exercise would not merely be 'imperfect' – it would be a vacuous attribute.

MAKING CLAIMS AND HAVING RIGHTS

Yet the special connection between rights and claims has been disputed, principally by White, on various grounds, several of which are important enough not to be left unattended.[2] White's thesis is that claims neither imply nor are implied by rights. To make a claim, so runs his first objection, is quite unconnected with having a right, since to claim a right is no different from claiming countless other things, such as knowledge, experience, an umbrella or any other *res*. This overlooks that, assuming the claim to be at least *prima facie* valid, the criteria of validity are quite different depending on what is claimed. If I claim fair or only little knowledge, the alleged degree is empirically verifiable; but where I claim an umbrella, I either have a claim or not, exactly according to whether or not I have a right to call the umbrella mine. Of course where I merely claim knowledge about a matter of fact, such a claim does not entail rights for the simple reason that it is a claim that something is or is not the case; except that even here claiming to have knowledge, rather than merely alleging or suggesting to have it, somehow advances a right to be believed or that one has grounds for saying one is knowledgeable. But performative claims do involve rights more directly, since these are claims especially designed to enable one to obtain or recover certain benefits.

Even if I do not claim a right as such, a claim is always for a right to a *res*, a payment, a patent, or a lost purse; for unless you have that right, you would have no justifiable claim and so be in no position to recover. If you claim not just your umbrella, but also your right to it, you are in fact claiming doubly, demanding its retention or recovery as well as affirming your ownership in the thing very emphatically. Sometimes, again, you may claim a benefit by claiming a certain status. To claim to be the long-lost heir is not merely to describe oneself, on good evidence, as the legitimate firstborn, it is also a claim to an estate which the rules of inheritance give to the claimant to the exclusion of younger or illegitimate offspring.

A second objection of White's deals with some alleged peculiarities of right. There are rights, he maintains, which would look undeniably dubious if treated as claims. Though we can have a right to laugh, to expect, or to feel pleased or indignant, it would be absurd to advance these as claims.[3] But there is here no real absurdity. To say 'you have every right to feel pleased', to take this now as representative, can be interpreted as meaning, for example that nobody can possibly accuse you of being arrogant if you feel pleased after your performance. Indeed unless we interpret the right to feel pleased in this way, as a defence against possible criticism, there would be little sense of speaking of a *right* to feel pleased. Nor would it be strange to say that, having a right to feel pleased, one can therefore claim to be allowed to feel pleased, or claim to remain unmolested or uncriticised if one so feels. For this 'right' (to feel pleased, or indignant, and so on) is here meant to state that one *may* feel pleased, not *why* one does. If a right to feel pleased merely conveyed one's pleased elation, this would have little to do with claims and rights; the person feeling pleased would only be doing what (to him) comes naturally.

White's other objections further insist that we should not confuse what is right to do or have with what one *has* a right to have. It may be only right, this objection goes, for me to sacrifice myself for another without its being my right to make such a sacrifice, while the fact that I have a right to chastise my son may not make it right for me to do so. These cases, too, are more easily explained. The father, in the latter case, can make no claim to punish his child if in certain circumstances this threatens to be neither right nor justifiable; this is because the father has only a limited right (in fact a discretionary right or power as more fully explained in Chapter 6) which he would exceed or abuse were he to exercise it unjustifiably; although subject to this he does retain a claim to punish on the basis of his parental right. As for the supererogatory self-sacrificer in the first case, his position is that acting heroically as he does, would admittedly not give him rights or claims against others, yet (and this is the point) would still give him a claim to a 'defensive' right; for having acted rightly, as he is considered to have acted, would allow him a right to be defended or exculpated were he, posthumously, in any danger of being adjudged a malfeasant suicide.

One or two further objections seem more difficult, but they too can be overcome. In some cases, it is true, even 'having' a claim cannot help one towards a right, but this would be a very special claim, one we may describe as 'applicatory' in character. One immigrant, in another of White's examples, may have a stronger claim than another immigrant to enter the United Kingdom, even though neither has a right of entry.[4] Here, it should be clear, neither immigrant 'has' a full claim; not only do their claims compete with each other, both are subject to a government discretion under which either immigrant's right of entry is to be decided. Similar considerations apply to the case where only a few of those making competing claims on someone's time will have a claim to that time. Assuming that the competing claims are all equally justified, assuming also a limitation of time, some selection has to be made. As a result some claims, though no less justified, will remain unrealised, yet this is only because of the hard luck of a selective procedure that simply cannot satisfy all applicants. The fact remains that in stating their claims, the various applicants are stating claims to a right, fully realising that, in the nature of the case, only one or a few applicants can be successful.

The preceding objections, then, far from weakening, rather strengthen the view that claims and rights are importantly linked, provided we see this connection as both propositional and performative. The link is crucial since this is our only means of obtaining a right, of asking for something as of right, without which rights would simply not confer what lawyers call actionable benefits, actionable in the sense of giving us an effective claim to a thing or benefit together with a claim upon or against another individual. Normative performatives, it will be noticed, cannot operate without such claims against, for concerned as such claims are with what we *may* do or have, they immediately draw attention to a second party as one of the necessary constituents of a right-relation. And though, as we have also seen, the word claim is by no means our only performative, as we can equally demand or request our rights, what distinguishes the latter is that, unlike claims, we cannot use them propositionally; the word claim implies, as other words do not, that it rests on some valid or 'rightful' ground: 'We claim this money' is like demanding it because we think or somehow are sure that we have a right to it. This is not to deny that 'right' and 'claim' remain different words: only rights can be enjoyed or exercised, only claims can be made or made out or met. Even so, it is not surprising that dictionaries often rely on 'claim' to define a right, or on 'right' to define a claim, for they are words which, despite their other differences, are so closely connected in doing their respective normative jobs as to require each other to make sense of each other: they constitute a sort of logical pair.

CLAIMS AND ENTITLEMENTS

That rights and claims are importantly linked has been challenged in another way. McCloskey, in particular, has argued that rights are better seen as entitlements rather than claims against others: thus better seen as being primarily entitlements to certain things: to do, have or enjoy whatever it is.[5] The word entitlement, it is admitted, is not an altogether happy choice, being obviously circular (if entitled to *x*, I've a right to it; if I've a right, I'm entitled). Still, the word is not viciously circular since it is not used reductively, but only to give us another perspective, to remind us that rights do not always connect with duties or claims against. The entitlement-theory, more especially, seeks to stress that claims derive from rights, not rights from claims; hence a person's right to marry, or to trade, or to own property, depends on his entitlement to do this; only when so entitled, and so having a right, does he have a claim against others not to be interfered with in what he does or expects. No other word seems quite so helpful as this. To speak of a 'power' or 'capacity' would not do, for a right-holder's power or capacity to pursue or engage in an activity depends not on his being able or willing but on whether he is entitled so to act.

The entitlement-theory also directs attention to the fact that where a person asserts his right to marry or trade, what he asserts is a right to a certain activity as such, independently of any possible interference with this right, for he may as yet not even know the persons who would or might interfere with him or whether indeed there will be any such persons. My right to marry or to life is *my* right, not an infinite list of claims against an infinite number of persons, some of whom as yet unborn, and all of whom as yet unknown as identifiable wrong-doers.[6] This certainly raises an important point. General rights (what lawyers call rights *in rem*, rights against the world) offer a special feature as compared with special rights (or rights *in personam*) in which the person against whom the claim is made is a specific or known individual. So it is not quite enough to say, as some have said, that rights *in rem* not only give rise to negative duties, duties not to interfere or to forbear, but can be discharged 'at one stroke simply by minding [one's] own business', so that there is nothing 'paradoxical' or 'troublesome' in the idea that the whole world, present or future, comes under a duty not to interfere with me or my rightful activities.[7] Not enough because, as McCloskey argues, this is not what is at stake here. My right to grow roses in my garden does not contemplate a direct claim against an assignable person, although it by no means excludes an eventual claim against a potential trespasser. Similarly, my institutional right to use the facilities of a club springs from my entitlement as a member (the club rules entitling members to use the library, the restaurant, and so on), not because I can make claims against others. My primary interest therefore is in the activity I wish to pursue, in my freedom to do gardening or use club facilities, not in possible lawsuits against those who might interfere with me: there may never be a need for such lawsuits if in fact no such interferers ever materialise.

To this extent the entitlement-theory indeed stresses an important feature, yet one it would seem more particularly pertaining to what is more correctly called the primacy of rights. As will now be clearer, we cannot establish a claim against, or identify the individual the claim is to be against, unless we already know what it is that our right or claim is about, what it is that our claim is *to*, so as to give rise to a claim against someone. Thus general rights to life, limb and property must exist to support appropriate duties or claims against those who interfere with these rights. Rights, in other words, must exist prior to duties as there must be claims to before there can be claims against; obviously it is truer to say that I have a duty not to interfere with you because you have a right, not that I have a right because you have a duty not to interfere. A duty could not even arise if there were no right.

Still, if the entitlement-theory serves as something of a corrective, we must beware of overstating it. For all its correct emphasis on claims to as compared with claims against, the fact remains that we cannot even have an entitlement or right to something without also having a right against. In doing what he does, our previous gardener or club member is admittedly not so much exercising a right *against* as rather engaging in an activity, nor for that matter exercising a right *to* as doing what his pleasure is. But suppose the gardener did say he had a *right* to cut his roses: what would be the point of saying that? What would be the point of saying he were 'entitled' to this activity without mentioning any right against? The only answer is that in saying this he wishes to indicate that he can, or has the power or capacity to do the acts specified. For this, however, he would not need the word 'right' or 'entitlement', either being chiefly meant to convey a normative fact, that I *may*, not merely *can*, do *x*; which in turn means that in doing *x* I occupy a sort of special position *vis-à-vis* others, being, for the purpose of *x*-ing, protected against any impeding intervention by them. Thus to assert a right or an entitlement to *x* is to assert something different from having a mere 'ability' or 'power' with regard to *x*; the latter only indicates what I can, not what I may, do. The verb 'may' always involves other persons, whereas 'can' does not.

To speak, then, of one's right to life or one's right to grow roses only makes sense if this right is somehow disputed or attacked; to refer to a 'right' would make no sense if nobody ever cared about what you did. If nobody ever threatened your physical integrity, or your growing roses, you would not be exercising a right to life or gardening, you would simply enjoy doing what you do. To speak of a right as something distinctive is therefore to claim some protective immunity or exclusivity in relation to others as well. Even where one says 'I enjoy my right to take time off from work', or 'my right to a holiday', what one has in mind is not only one's right to but also rights against, for one is not just saying that one enjoys one's time off or one's holiday but also the right as such – that one enjoys the fact that employer or colleagues cannot really stop me from carrying on with my project as I wish. There is thus a clear difference between saying 'I shall enjoy my holiday', and 'I shall enjoy my right to a holiday', since the latter statement communicates a good deal more.

Nevertheless the temptation dies hard to regard entitlements as being so completely rights to as to obscure their being also rights correlative to duties, however remote or contingent these duties may be. There is, as we shall shortly see, a class of rights that indeed does not involve duties, being purely defensive rights. But the rights we now consider, which are also our paradigm of rights, are not of this type. Even so some ingenious arguments are sometimes advanced to prove the existence of 'dutiless' rights. McCloskey gives the example of the conscientious objector who refuses to obey a law he considers unjust, namely, a statute requiring him to abort a woman to save her life.[8] The objector, he contends, here has a right not to conform as he has a right to follow his own conscience, without there being a corresponding duty in anyone to respect this right; on the contrary, the statue expressly requires the opposite. But this example does not really convince. Insofar as the objector does have a moral right, that of refraining from certain actions on conscientious grounds, we, his fellow citizens, cannot but respect his non-conformity, whatever the state may do. The state can of course still punish the objector for doing that to which he has a moral right; but this only shows that the moral right conflicts with the commands of the legislature, not that the moral right has no correlative duty anywhere. Indeed, what sort of right would the conscientious objector have, or what would he be in a position to complain about as of right, if the moral right we do attribute to him could be disregarded with complete (uncritical) impunity? Surely it is only because his right of objection does assume some recognition, together with some duty against interference in the rest of us, that we can even speak of the objector's having a moral right rather than merely a moral view, or that we can speak of a conflict between the law of the state and an individual's moral right.

A cognate criticism applies to McCloskey's category of 'negative' rights which are similarly asserted to be dutiless.[9] His illustration is of the so-called right to build a sandcastle or dig a hole on the beach, rights in respect of which others may or may not have a duty not to interfere. Yet it is not easy to see what these 'negative' examples actually amount to. If the right to dig sand does go with some corresponding duty, the negative right seems as complete as any other 'dutiful' right. And if the right is not so protected, one wonders what the right can consist of; because if no duties whatever are involved, children playing in the sand would not be exercising a right but would simply be playing so long as they could. Once again, the conclusion is that entitlements cannot qualify as rights unless there are corresponding duties in or on others at least lurking in the background even if not immediately apparent or operative otherwise.

SUBJUNCTIVE CLAIMS

Though our main concern at present is with positive or established rights, we may briefly consider rights which, if not yet established, we nevertheless think to be eminently establishable on moral or legal grounds. Consider then claims which take a 'subjunctive' form, that is, claims or demands or requests that something be, or should be, the case.[10] Subjunctive claims must of course be distinguished from such earlier claims as those for a patent or old age pensions in which the deciding factor is chiefly factual, namely, whether the claimant has or has not complied with the rules (that of becoming a patentee in the one case, an old age pensioner in the other). The claims we are now considering are distinctly more argumentative, the main question being whether the claimant *should* have a benefit, for the reasons he gives. Thus in making a subjunctive claim I do not advance grounds which are propositionally true or false, but rather grounds which are just or unjust, fair or unfair, or justified or unjustified, always depending on the strength of the moral or legal considerations mustered for the claim. What such considerations might be we shall discuss at a later stage; yet it will already be clear that not all considerations or reasons we advance will be equally acceptable, for some may well be rejected as unjustified.

Nevertheless, even a subjunctive claim, if it is to be a claim and not just a view or opinion proffered to the world, must still make a *prima facie* case, or a case for a *prima facie* right; for unless I am making a false claim (either advancing the wrong facts or a wrong or irrelevant principle), or merely demanding instead of claiming, my claim would not be arguable, that is, accompanied by reasons which support or justify my claim, even if only partially. If there are reasons which are found to be weightier, my *prima facie* right will be overridden; if, however, my reasons are sound or tenable on principle, my claim will have some validity. Thus a claim for higher wages, though obviously admitting that one has as yet no (legal) right to them, nonetheless does emphasise that one is not just claiming what one wishes or demands to have, but that the claim is justified, at any rate justifiable, by relevant social or economic arguments. We have institutions to hear and then to accept or reject those arguments; but unless claims for higher wages or similar benefits did contemplate possible rights, or rights one ought to have along the lines of the claims, it would be difficult to understand why claims would be made at all. What is more, once the relevant procedures have been gone through, it is conceded that one does have a moral claim, one would, by the same token, have a moral and normally also a legal right. The legal right, admittedly, might still become inoperative; but this would then only mean either that the claims through which certain rights were pressed have now changed their procedures or tests of justification, or that the rights have been cancelled by political fiat irrespective of the arguments supporting them.

From this perspective we can better approach Feinberg's well-known example of the sickly, hungry, orphaned child for whom you cannot help but feel pity and more.[11] Does not this child, he asks, have a *claim* to be fed and housed? Will we not still believe it even if we despair of finding anyone whose duty it is to provide these things? And if we finally do assign the duty to someone, will we not do so only because there is a prior claim, a claim to being fed, and so on, arising directly from the child's needs? Such claims he calls 'inchoate' or 'manifesto' rights, or claims which are like 'the natural seed from which rights grow'.[12] It can, however, be a little misleading to put the matter just in this way. An impression is created that one can have a claim, even an apparently valid claim, as distinct from a right. If claims are merely humanitarian pleas for assisting deprived human beings, then they are certainly not rights but neither are they properly claims; at best they are demands for rights. If, on the other hand, we take claims more strictly, especially when we say that someone has a 'valid' claim, one (let us say) fully justified by moral principle, such a claim, as we earlier argued, cannot but be tantamount to a right. This, to be sure, still does not explain when, or by what moral standard, a moral claim can be adjudged as valid or justified; we still need criteria to be able to assess moral claims, criteria which the claim itself does not provide. Precisely this difficulty will later lead us to re-examine the problem of natural or moral rights.

2 Rights as Defences and Liberties

DEFENSIVE RIGHTS: THEIR GENERAL CHARACTER

The concept of right, we already hinted, carries elements which allow for two quite distinct senses: one which interlocks with claims both to and against, and a second sense which also affirms one's claim or right to act in a certain way, yet does so without asserting a duty on the other side or claim against. Such is a right of self-defence, or a right to criticise, or to divorce or separate, or to terminate a contract, or to give notice to a tenant, or the right to compete in trade, or the right to picket.[1] We shall call these defensive rights, sometimes called liberties or liberty-rights, to distinguish them from rights with correlative duties or fully assertive rights.

Rights operate defensively if used not as claims against, but as defences to complaints or grievances from another. For I can claim that I *may* do *x*, or have a right to do it, and say this by way of a justification or excuse or defence, whenever I am confronted by some moral or legal charge that my action has harmed or hurt another. Such a defence, it must be noticed, is far from independent of duties; its function is to qualify my duty towards another and, concomitantly, his rights against me. This shows the defensive right to be not a denial of the right–duty relationship, but rather a gloss on it – a gloss required where normal right–duty relations are somehow inverted, as in (a major example) the right of self-defence. As a general rule, *A*, like the rest of us, is under a duty not to do harm to *B* while *B* is under the same duty to *A*. Suppose that *A* attacks *B*, threatening *B*'s life in so instant and decisive a manner as to deny *B* any opportunity of calling for official help, thus leaving him no option but to defend himself as best he can. In these circumstances *A*'s own right against harm must be qualified or at least diminished in relation to *B*; for *B* becomes entitled to defend himself, and in so doing to inflict such damage on *A* as to stop the clear and present danger to himself.

However to say that *B* now has a right of self-defence is not so much to enable him to protect himself (this, we may suppose, *B* will do anyhow to the best of his ability), but to give *B* a defence or excuse if *A* were to complain that *B* caused him serious injury. This right so attributed to *B* cannot be described as a normal claim against *A*, but it can be described as a claim in which *B* is affirming that, given the clear and present danger created by *A*, he (*B*) may do things he would be under a duty not to do otherwise.

At the other end of the scale, there is the more familiar situation in which a person suffers hurt only because he voluntarily exposes himself to it. If *B* freely submits to dental surgery by *A, B* has nothing to complain about however unpleasant *A*'s ministrations are. *A*'s defense simply is that *B* expressly consented to the pain, his consent thus vacating any injury, something which lawyers usually describe as *volenti non fit injuria*, a maxim which expresses as much of a moral as a legal principle. Not that this principle is without bounds. It always depends on what the consent is for, or for what kind of injury; not all injuries can be agreed to by the victim – only such, broadly speaking, which can be said to correspond to his interest. Selling oneself into slavery, or selling one's limbs for commercial purposes would be an illegitimate and therefore voidable consent. We shall have to say more about this at a later stage.

More interesting at present are cases in which a person gives his implicit rather than explicit consent: as where he (publicly) exposes himself to conduct by others with adverse effects on him. Take the situation where *A* criticises *B*'s performance at a public concert or criticises *B*'s novel offered for public review. Such criticism often tends to become starkly personal since the criticism is not generally directed at the work of art but at the artist or author himself, with the innuendo that he could or should have done better than he did.[2] Now unless a person actually exposes himself to such criticism, he enjoys an immunity against being criticised, at least by strangers, however competent or informed the latter may be. The reason is that unless criticism is somehow invited, adverse comment about somebody else's work can be most insulting, gratuitously so, to the person concerned. Just as a person has a right not to be harmed physically or economically, so he has a right not to have his feelings hurt or to be publicly shamed or ridiculed. A stranger cannot just go and tell another, *coram publico* and in a loud voice, that he looks ugly or deformed, for even if true, this would be an unfortunate fact, not an occasion for criticism. The stranger's conduct may also amount to a legal wrong such as perhaps an extended form of defamation or invasion of privacy, but even if not legally actionable it would still constitute conduct that is morally reprehensible, thus liable to moral censure, being conduct undertaken for no better reason than personal offensiveness.

The situation is very different where comment or criticism is clearly invited, not just gratuitous. In relationships such as between teacher and pupil or parent and child, the teacher or parent not only has a right to criticise but the pupil or child is under a duty to listen, though even so under no further duty to suffer public exposure. Others, as our aforementioned artist or author, have not the same duty to listen, but they are bound to submit to public comment; for having exposed themselves as public figures, any competent member of the public can exercise his right to criticise just as he can exercise his right of free speech on a public issue, even if the persons criticised are deeply offended. If the latter now voice a legal or moral complaint, the critic can plead a defence known as fair comment; that is, he can say that he *may* criticise another even to the extent of hurting his feelings, without thereby doing wrong, if the circumstances are such that people should be free to exercise their judgment about an act or performance that invites social comment or approval, always provided the judgment is informed or at any rate in good faith, for if not, the critic could turn out to be merely malicious rather than genuinely critical.

RIGHTS AND LIBERTIES

Defensive rights are often described as liberties or liberty-rights, a denomination which has however given rise to a great deal of theoretical confusion. A long-standing view in fact is that liberties represent not, as we shall suggest, essentially defensive rights, but represent permissions of a more complexly special kind. This view comes in various versions, and it is important to come to terms with them one by one.

For Raphael, to begin with philosophically perhaps the best-known version, a liberty is a 'right of action', a right which affirms our freedom or licence to do something: to sing in the bath, cultivate one's garden, or give away one's inheritance, without there being any moral or legal obligation to refrain from these actions.[3] This liberty is distinguished from a 'right of recipience' which is the right to receive something from someone, including the advantage of being left alone.

Whereas a recipient right constitutes a right *to* liberty, a right of action is rather *a* liberty, a permissive right or licence to do one's own thing, free from contrary obligations. Several difficulties appear immediately. A basic one is that the liberty or right of action emerges as not very much of a right if we re-examine the examples on which it is based. How can there be a liberty-right, say, to sing in the bath, unless there is also a recipient right not to be interfered with while the song is sung. Raphael admits that where a man has a right of action he usually has *in addition* a right of recipience to be left alone, provided he can show that his proposed action is neither wrong nor unlawful, for if wrong he could not have a recipient right to be secure in what he does. Raphael further admits that we do not normally speak of rights of action, unless we are hindered by others in exercising them. Even as regards so-called 'universal human rights', such as the right to work or the right to seek asylum, we try to convey not that working or seeking asylum are permissible, but that such rights or claims should *be allowed*; for, as Raphael rightly observes, a mere declaration of a right to work would be pointless if all it meant was that there is nothing wrong in work or that there should be no law forbidding it: hence to claim a right to work is to claim not a liberty, only a right *to* liberty, namely, a positive opportunity to work.[4]

If so, the next question is when, and how, a right of action would be operative independently, without the addition of a recipient right? For, as we are also told, while one cannot have a recipient right without a prior right of action, the latter does not depend on the former, since a right of action can exist independently; it is legitimate to describe a person as having a right or liberty to do certain things, or having an exemption not to act, without it being necessary to add a recipient right against interference. But if so, what becomes or remains of the liberty-right or right of action? Sometimes, of course, we may merely wish to report the existence of such a right of action: that, for example, we now have a right or liberty we did not have previously. Again, and nearer our case, we may wish to deny that a particular action or forbearance (singing or not singing in the bath) is unlawful or morally wrong. But such a denial is not where, in relation to rights, the matter ends; for, given the normative context in which words like right or liberty operate, the real point of denying that an action is unlawful or wrong is to give someone a defence to a complaint that might be raised against him. To say, in other words, that one *may* do *x*, or is free to do it, is precisely to deny another a legal or moral claim he might otherwise have against one.

This is not all. Since on the above account a right of action does not envisage a defensive right, nor for that matter an assertive right (as our terms of reference now include the right of action but exclude a right of recipience), we are left with this dilemma: either, on a stricter interpretation of Raphael, the right of action merely indicates an action not morally or legally proscribed, in which case however any non-proscribed action (sleeping, walking, having breakfast, and so on) becomes a liberty or right, which cannot have been the result here intended. Or, on a wider interpretation, the right of action literally disappears as a right since, in the absence of any assertive or defensive function, there is nothing for the so-called 'right' to be a right about. If, to take this second case through a somewhat banal example, someone claimed to have a right to kick that stone, a stone (let us assume) belonging to nobody, such that its being kicked could never be taken as unlawful or wrong, what sort of 'right' would the kicker be stating to have? Admittedly, the kicker *can* do what he does; but to say that he *may* kick that stone would be only worth stating in a normative sense, if somebody did deny or even doubt his right to kick, that is, a sense that either supports a claim to kick or offers a defence to a complaint about kicking the stone.

Nor is the last difficulty resolved or even avoided by another example of Raphael's, the example of *A*'s kicking his child downstairs, and *C*, a bystander, telling *A*: 'You have no right to kick the boy'.[5] Here, it should be obvious, the bystander as well as condemning *A* is also telling him that he lacks any possible defence for what he is doing and that, without such a defence, nothing can reduce the child's normal (recipient) right not to be injured so wantonly. This example does to some extent support the view that a right may operate defensively; but it does nothing to assist Raphael's thesis that a liberty or a liberty-right represents an independent species of right, one without any other normative implications than that a particular act is not unlawful or wrong. Indeed to disregard all wider normative implications leads to profound misconceptions as to the very nature of a right or even a liberty. As we have seen, an activity to sing in the bath can be pursued *ad libitum*, provided one has a voice and a bath. Except that the question then arises of why this 'can' should be called a right, since the 'can' here refers to a purely physical ability to act in a certain way.[6] If, however, we concede that a right or liberty involves an assertion that one *may* or is *free* to act in a certain way, this implies a two-party relation with other claims or defences, since to say I *may* sing in the bath is to assert either that I be allowed to sing where others wish to prevent me, or that I have a good defence where others are complaining about my noise.

Unless, moreover, this normative 'may' is distinguished from the physical 'can', we cannot even begin to trace the logical outlines of a right, for only the 'may' connects with a permissive function, irrespective of whether one can or not. A blind man cannot see but he still has a right to see; an infirm person can be incapacitated from voting, but he has a right to vote. Similarly to say that a person is 'unfree' to act is not just to say that he is unable to do what he desires to do, for this would suggest that he might be free if he did not have a particular desire. Hence one's lack of liberty can only be gauged by such untoward action by others as prevents one from doing what one might otherwise be able to do, even if one has no desire to do it. If detained in the grandest palace I would still be unfree to go into the street, whether I wanted to or not. Thus the facts of freedom depend on actual prevention to exercise it, not on one's personal judgments about the desirable scope of how it should be exercised. As before, therefore, if freedom is to be a right, we are at once involved in a two-party relationship.

LIBERTIES: OTHER VERSIONS

The view that liberties constitute a separate species of rights has been advanced in two other versions with more legal overtones. A liberty, Glanville Williams has maintained, is a purely negative concept, while a right includes something that can be claimed; a right exists where there is a positive law on the subject, unlike a liberty where there is no law against it; in short, a right is correlative to a duty, whereas a liberty is not, it merely denies or abrogates an obligation to do or not to do.[7] Thus the liberty to walk along the street is an expression of the absence of any law against my walking, it does not reflect a duty not to stop me walking, for there is no such duty apart from the wider duty not to commit assault. In this way, liberties and rights become, for Williams, quite different notions: different because a liberty only means that I don't commit a tort or other delict in doing a given act whereas a right does mean that a tort or offence is committed if I am interfered with doing this. Different, too, because liberty and right relate to contrary things: I may have a liberty to do something without having a correlative right against interference. So a liberty acquires an entirely neutral quality, in that conduct one is at liberty to do does not require approval, whether in law or in morality: *non omne quod licet honestum est*.[8]

The right–liberty distinction, as Williams adumbrates it, is however more radical still. We are invited to regard an alleged 'right' as a right in a strict sense if, and only if, it has an exactly corresponding correlative to it. A familiar right such as a right of way is therefore not a right since there is no 'duty of way', the servient owner having no duty to provide a way. A right of way thus turns out to be no more than a 'liberty of way', albeit a liberty combined with an ordinary right not to have the way obstructed or its user assaulted. But if a liberty requires a right against obstruction, what, we may ask, is the liberty about, for is not the admitted right against obstruction precisely what a right of way is concerned with? Even more surprising is Williams's example of the lunatic. If the latter attacks a man, yet is held to be not liable for lack of mental or moral responsibility, his attack is now said to be 'legally the exercise of a liberty', although the person attacked has the 'liberty' of self-defence. Surely even a lunatic can be said to remain under a duty not to attack or harm anyone, however unenforceable that duty may be in fact. In any event, the person attacked has not merely a 'liberty' but has a 'right' of self-defence. Nor is this a minor terminological difference; for should the person attacked, acting in reasonable self-defence, injure the lunatic, the latter or those representing him would be met by an effective plea of justification for any injury that might result. The right of self-defence is here the same as that previously described, a right one is entitled to exercise in order to defend onself.

Williams's other examples are no more supportive of his categorisation of 'liberties'. Take his two people trying to pick up a seemingly ownerless gold watch first. If you pick it up first, you interfere with my liberty, but not with my right, for you do not commit a tort in picking it up before I can. A little reflection shows that you and I have here more than mere liberties, if only because we also have mutual rights and duties to afford each other equally unobstructed opportunities in our competitive race for the watch. A similar point applies to an ordinary commercial competition between rival traders, each of whom tries to clinch a profitable deal with a third. In a number of cases, so the criticism goes, courts have talked of every person's right or liberty to trade freely, usually employing the words right and liberty interchangeably, without apparently realising that they committed a fallacy, that of converting a mere 'liberty' to trade into a full-fledged 'right'.[9] But where, if we look again, is the alleged fallacy? In this sort of situation, the trader competing has a defensive right to pursue his business even if it hurts another in the same trade (this is, after all, what competition here means); however the trader so hurt does have an assertive right to complain, if the former can be said to have not just competed but to have unduly or improperly interfered with his own right to trade. On Williams's own definition, it is difficult to see why the latter trader has a mere liberty; what he is claiming is not just greater freedom but fair conduct on the other side. The traders now accused of unfair competition might well speak of *their* liberty to compete freely, liberty thus becoming the same as a defensive right, although in situations of conflicting rights as we have here the question of whether the defendant trader has a defence coincides with the question of whether the plaintiff has a claim: for both answers here depend on what, in such competitive situations, the scope of fair as against unfair trading is to be.[10]

Another version of liberty-rights is that propounded by Hart. For him, indeed, liberties have a very central significance as they lie analytically at the heart of all legal rights. Describing liberties as Bentham did, namely, as rights arising from the absence of any legal prohibition or arising from permissive or discoercive laws, Hart begins with an interesting example of a man looking at his neighbour over the garden fence.[11] The former is under no obligation to look or not to look; the neighbour, too, has no correlative obligation to let himself be looked at: he could, for example, erect a screen on his land. But Hart's broader point is that *A* here has a liberty to look at *B*, however tormenting *B* may find *A*'s gaze, although *B* has no duty to submit to such looking as though he were his debtor or obligor.

This argument is seriously flawed. In particular it seems to overlook that a person is by no means free to exercise his vision for the sole purpose of tormenting others if his looking at them is indeed capable of being significantly offensive or hurtful to them. Of course *A* has a right to exercise his vision in the same way as he has the right to use his land or property. If *A* grows trees on his land which *B* deeply dislikes, *B* is nevertheless bound to respect this 'natural' exercise of *A*'s property rights. Very similarly, *A* can exercise what can be called his visual property by looking at *B* without *B* being able to stop *A* from doing so. For *A* would here be doing a normal and natural act: looking at people in one's field of vision is something we cannot really avoid. Here *A* would therefore have a good defence were *B* to complain; and to this defensive extent *A* would have a right or a liberty. The position is however very different where *A* overdoes or abuses this right, by looking at *B* not just naturally but with an unconcealed intention of being intrusive or 'tormenting' to *B*. For here *B* will have at least a moral claim to complain about *A*'s conduct towards him, simply on the ground that *A*'s unceasing gaze constitutes a discomforting and insufferable intrusion for which *A* has no justifying defence. Indeed, *B* might also have, or contend for, legal redress, even if there is as yet no specific delict covering such harm; but there are no insuperable obstacles to prevent such conduct from becoming legally actionable, at least through an injunction to stop *A* from visually interfering with *B*. The long and short of this is that, if *A*'s gaze is intentionally tormenting, or deliberately offends *B*'s normal sensibilities, *A*'s conduct would no longer be a liberty-right but become a breach of a duty not to interfere. It follows that tormenting another, if only by visual action, cannot be a liberty or liberty-right simply because it is not an action which a person may do as a matter of right.

Nor is Hart on safer ground with another argument. Those who think that liberty-rights are not worth our attention because they are not really protected rights do not, he suggests, fully appreciate that liberty-rights are in fact well enough protected, albeit indirectly rather than directly, by 'a protective perimeter behind which liberties exist and may be exercised'. A trivial example is my right to scratch my head – a right protected not by a correlative obligation upon others not to interfere with my scratching, but by the more comprehensive obligations to refrain from interfering with my person or my activities as a person.[12] This is somewhat reminiscent of Williams's aforementioned views of the right (or liberty) of way; but however this may be, Hart does not really explain why, logically or conceptually, we should regard such a liberty as surrounded by a 'perimeter' rather than look at it more straightforwardly as a right with a correlative duty. Interfering with my scratching is not only an unwarranted invasion of personal freedom but, as well, one of the countless interferences that come within the ambit of trespass or similar offences, whether in civil or criminal law. However Hart is insistent that we should not allow the protective perimeter to obscure a view of liberty that sees it as an absence of obligation, if only because, he argues, others could still interfere with my scratching my head, or any other personal action of mine, without any breach of an obligation – for example, by hypnotising me. This contention would be alarming if it were really true. If I am hypnotised against my wish, can one say there is no breach of at least a moral obligation not to tamper with me as a person or with my mental autonomy? If I am hypnotised with my consent, there is of course no comparable breach, at least to the extent to which the rule of *volenti non fit injuria* now obtains; but, in any case, the hypnotiser would now be acting with the other's permission, not in pursuance of a liberty.

At another point in Hart's discussion the distinction between rights and liberties is left so thin as to make what remains of it scarcely viable. Discussing the case of two parties racing for a purse they both see lying in the street, Hart maintains, like Williams before him, that each party has a liberty to pick up the purse, but then, unlike Williams, also concedes that there are specific things which each has a right the other should not do, for there are rights with correlative obligations which protect and also restrict each party's liberty.[13] So where Williams saw an unbridgeable cleavage between liberties and ordinary rights, Hart rushes upon the opposite mistake of constructing what he thinks appropriate bridges between them. If liberties have to be surrounded by such protective perimeters of correlative rights and duties, what is the point of having liberties as distinct from rights? For if there is to be a perimeter to provide the necessary 'ring' within which a liberty can be exercised, it is difficult to see what exactly that liberty amounts to as a separate concept. In the example above each party is said to be 'at liberty' to pick up the purse, even to pick it up first; but this is a liberty not only subject to certain conditions which the aforementioned obligations try to express – the so-called liberty to run for and pick up the purse is simply nothing more than a defensive right if one of the runners challenges the other asking by what right he is competing with him.

A REVISED DICHOTOMY OF RIGHTS

The previous criticisms were not intended to bury the liberty-right, only to rescue it, now within conceptually firmer boundaries. The boundaries proposed confine the liberty to a predominantly defensive role, to be used as a right in situations where *A*'s action proves detrimental to *B* but where *A* nevertheless has a defence, on the ground that he (*A*) may act in the way he does even if his actions adversely affect *B*, as where *B* suffers injury, whether in his person or his property or his standing in society. Not that *A*'s justificatory defence is here seen as superior to *B*'s complaint, or that *B*'s harm is seen as inferior to *A*'s, the position rather is that *A*'s defence arises because *B* can be said to have, directly or indirectly, exposed himself to the harm.

To confine liberties or liberty-rights in the manner proposed may also offer a more coherent conceptual map, one in which 'liberty', varied as that word is, can nevertheless be given a more independent sense. For this very reason we earlier distinguished assertive from defensive rights, the latter, unlike the former, not giving rise to a claim against. Unless indeed we make such a distinction, it is difficult to see how we can both preserve the liberty as a right and yet differentiate it effectively from (Hohfeld's) claim-right or (Raphael's) recipient right. It does not seem to have been noticed that if a liberty is given a more assertive sense, it collapses into a claim-right, leaving no work for the liberty as a separate (or defensive) right; and if a liberty is merely taken to denote a right arising from the absence of a legal duty or prohibition, as it now commonly is, only telling us what we *may* do henceforth, that 'may' must also refer to others: that, more exactly, we *may* speak freely or sing in the bath, however much neighbours or others object. In either case the result is that we are again enmeshed in a right–duty relationship, in that there is now another side that is at least morally, and possibly even legally, bound to let us exercise the alleged liberty. The same point can be made in Hohfeldian terms. To state that *A* has a privilege or liberty of action means, according to Hohfeld, that *B* has a correlative 'no-right'. Thus if *A* has a liberty to walk on *B*'s grass, *B* has a no-right concerning *A*'s walking on the grass. Yet to say that *B* has a no-right must (for reasons we more fully explain in Chapter 5) imply that *B* is under a duty not to interfere, for this is the only way in which a no-right can take effect, if we agree that a no-right is to serve a normative function, not just to stand as a pure and simple denial of the word 'right'.

Loose as our linguistic usages are, the temptation has long been to give the word liberty very wide scope. The temptation has been to assume that since one can use 'right' without any reference to corresponding duties, this use is best rendered by the word liberty. Liberty thus began to be seen as a sort of purely personal, because 'dutiless', right to act exactly according to our interests. Where ordinary rights, or claim-rights, so it has seemed, protect us mainly in our person or property, liberties or liberty-rights rather extend or expand our capacity to act, giving us new opportunities to work, to create, to amass wealth, or pursue courses of action that realise our human potentialities. It should now be clearer that this impression is quite wrong. Assertive or recipient rights, too, safeguard the pursuit of such liberties. In fact the whole purpose of these rights is to protect us not alone in our physical integrity, or our property, but also in our personal autonomy to enable us to achieve our material or other self-realising ends. Recipient rights protect us precisely because they provide claims against actual or even merely possible interferences by others; they are indeed our primary or basic rights. Unless we do have such rights to begin with, there would be no point in talking about liberties or defensive rights, simply because there would be no right–duty relationships defensive rights could connect with, for it is right–duty relationships that defensive rights presuppose or depend on for their own operation as rights.

3 Rights, Benefits and Interests

BENEFITS AND INTERESTS

Our discussion of rights as claims or entitlements, or as defences or liberties, has taken us some distance, but we have still quite a way to go, if only to consider still other elements that conceptually form part of rights. Our next question will chiefly be this: if rights are claims *to* something, what, very generally, can this something be? As one can claim many things – to live, or to be safe, or to marry, or to ply one's trade – it is clear that what a person is claiming (we assume, for the present, always against another individual) will comprise some benefit or advantage or, more broadly, an interest he wishes to realise. Of course not every personal benefit one wants or claims qualifies automatically as a right. But a right, so we shall now argue, must contain at least an element of benefit to be a right at all. To make a claim to something means that the claimant seeks something he deems beneficial or of interest to himself: only so can its denial to him constitute a ground for complaint. For, normally, one only complains because one has been deprived of some benefit; if a particular benefit were not missed one would have no grievance. One cannot complain if one finds oneself better instead of worse off. For greater clarity we shall first discuss benefits, later interests.

It goes without saying that the word benefit must be used in a conventional rather than too literal sense. A claimant, for example, may not in actual fact benefit from money given or repaid to him as he may waste it on drink. Yet he can still say that getting his money back is beneficial to him, or is in his interest; hence the purposes on which he perhaps 'wastes' his money do not affect the benefit he has in recovering what is his; the benefit lies in getting back his own money like any other creditor. Were a debtor able to impose what he himself might consider to be beneficial to his creditor, the latter would not be left with much of a personal benefit, let alone a complete or unqualified right.[1] Even where a debtor does not pay back money, so that the creditor does not actually benefit, this still does not affect the use of the word, for it is sufficient that the claimant would benefit. Indeed claims are made precisely because the claimant does not yet but still wishes to have that benefit; only because the debtor withholds the benefit does the creditor press the right.

Neither does a benefit have to consist of positive gains or increments; the benefit may be purely negative, such as the benefit of being left alone, or of not being interfered with in one's person or property. In many cases, admittedly, the benefit sought relates to positive performances rather than negative forbearances; but 'benefit' easily extends to negative acts simply because a person complaining of an interference with his body or things is plainly complaining of being deprived of an omission eminently beneficial to him. On the other hand, a murderer sentenced to be hanged cannot be said to have a true benefit in having his sentence executed; accordingly he has no 'right' to be punished, and he has no such right not so much because the executioner does not 'serve' the murderer, being rather an agent of the state, as because it seems absurd to say that the murderer is claiming something for his benefit. Rights and benefits thus emerge as analytically interrelated; without a benefit a person would have nothing personal to claim for himself; there would be no link or nexus between the claim and the right.

It is sometimes still maintained, however, that rights also arise independently of benefits. A person, it is said, can have rights of which he is unaware: he may have acquired a legacy without knowing he has, or like a child be intellectually incapable of appreciating that he has benefits of any kind. But the former ignorance only shows that if one does not know certain facts one will lose out on a beneficial right, the regret being precisely that one loses out on a benefit, just as one's mental incapacity makes it the more important for another to represent the former's rights just because personal benefits are involved. Similarly it is sometimes maintained that rights are not always beneficial since one may have a right to enter a burning building or eat poisoned food; these, certainly, would be strange rights to claim, unless for purely professional reasons (as by a fireman or a professional taster of food); but even if claimed by others we may still assume that they must regard such acts as, to them, beneficial options enabling them to take high risks with their lives without interference from anyone. Again it has been argued, increasingly so in recent times, that benefit cannot be an appropriate test for rights especially in relation to animals who it is alleged also have rights even if they lack any understanding of their benefits. But animals present a special – and we shall see (in Chapter 10) a somewhat marginal – difficulty. For the present our main concern is with what we take as our paradigm case, that of the normal adult person who will not have or acquire rights unless he claims those rights and who will not claim rights without thereby seeking some benefit to himself, a benefit understood as such by people at large.

THE BENEFIT-THEORY: OBJECTIONS I

The close connection of rights with benefits has nevertheless been strongly disputed even for our paradigm case. There are ordinary rights, it is objected, which are not essentially beneficial at all. The benefit-theory, the argument goes, though adequate for many situations, yet fails to give a complete account of rights. In civil law rights have a force independent of benefit, civil rights now being taken as the litmus test for rights in general. Professor Hart, the main protagonist of this view, rests this objection on the ground that the benefit-theory obscures the nature of *relative* duties, the duties arising in civil law (say, tort or contract) as distinct from the absolute duties we find in criminal law.[2] Relative duties have this particular feature of giving a right-holder a sort of 'normative property' which he is in full control of, and so is in a position to modify or waive the right as he alone thinks fit. It is this latter option, not the fact that he stands to benefit, that, for Hart, makes it appropriate to say that a person has a right; only rights one can modify or waive or cancel, which one thus 'owns', or has a 'limited sovereignty' in, are therefore rights in a strict sense. In the criminal law, where the duties are absolute, the right-holder has no corresponding rights since the duties there are not similarly within his control, but are enforced as a matter of public policy.

One immediate question is why a right-holder endowed with normative property should be denied to have a benefit; for is that property not of benefit to him? There are other criticisms as well. It does not seem very convincing to regard criminal law as not giving rise to rights when its aim is surely to protect a person's rights just as does civil law. Admittedly there is the difference of some criminal offences not being privately waivable, as they can always be prosecuted by any member of the public or an appropriate official agency. This however does not alter the right: the unwaivability only makes the right protectively stronger, making it, in the classical phrase, into an inalienable right.[3] Hart does concede that some criminal-law duties, especially those for the protection of the individual other than duties relating to, for example, military service, might be said to give rise to 'rights' – rights in a colloquial yet still 'tolerable' sense. But if so what can be meant by 'tolerable'? If this is to be no more than a purely verbal concession, this becomes an odd way of describing some of our most basic rights, such as our rights to life, limb and property. And if intended to be more than merely verbal, this would in effect undermine Hart's whole argument; for he would now admit as rights even those not purely waivable or modifiable by the parties themselves.

Hart's discussion does draw attention to the fact that there are rights, like absolute or inalienable ones, which are not quite so freely optional as other rights; that unlike purely civil rights which may, or may not, be exercised, there are some rights which cannot be abandoned – like the right to vote which, as in Australia, is made compulsory. This again, however, does not weaken but rather strengthens the benefit-theory. Some rights can now be seen as being so basic and hence so much in need of protection as not to be waivable at all. A person not exercising his basic right seems as much in need of protection as is a child; others must intervene to exercise, or make him exercise, his rights for him. Even the voter, where voting is compulsory, can still be said to have a right rather than a duty: he has a (to him) beneficial right which he cannot be deprived of, also a right entitling him to vote according to his choice. What distinguishes such a voter from, for example, a taxpayer is that the latter is under a duty to comply with the revenue laws, hence not in the least describable as 'beneficially entitled' to pay his taxes, whereas the voting citizen may complain if his voting right is interfered with; for this would tamper with a personal benefit in that it would seriously affect his social a political position in the community he is supposed to be a full member of. Indeed, as we shall see (more fully in Chapter 8), our most important rights are unwaivable or inalienable precisely in this way, being mostly rights not fully optional, rather rights entitling one to benefits one has no permission to abandon or alienate.

THE BENEFIT-THEORY: OBJECTIONS II

Still further objections have been raised to show that rights can be dissociated from benefits. One such, also from Hart, uses a contractual example drawn from current English law which involves three persons: *A* promising *B* to pay a sum of money to *C*.[4] Here the contention is that *B* has the right but no real benefit, while *C* has the benefit but no right. Now it is true that the law still regards *C* as a 'stranger' to the obligation from *A* to *B*; even so, it seems odd to treat *B* as having no benefit or *C* as totally rightless. Why, for one thing, would *B* wish to 'buy' a promise from *A* for the support of *C*; unless *B* is seen as deriving at least some satisfaction from seeing *C* supported, the arrangement would make no sense for him. *B*'s satisfaction or benefit may be sentimental, while *C*'s interest may be material or monetary in the main; this however does not alter the fact that *B*'s benefit is nonetheless a real one; *A*'s promise obviously concerns him, a promise which *B* may have gone to great trouble to obtain. Furthermore, *C*'s position is not quite so rightless as presented here. *C*, it is suggested, has the benefit but no right because it is only to *B* that *A*'s promise is due since *B* alone can waive the claim; thus it is *B* who is wronged but not harmed while, on the other hand, it is *C* who is harmed but not wronged. Consequently only the promisee (*B*) has a claim against *A* as *B* alone is in a position to waive or press the claim, and it is this, not *B*'s benefit, that gives him the right.

How strong is this as a moral argument? Suppose *C* is *B*'s mother in need of support, and that *C* is aware that *A* made this promise for her benefit. Surely *C* has a moral claim if only because of her justified expectation of support. As the one intended beneficiary of *A*'s promise to *B*, *C* will be seriously harmed if *A* deliberately fails to keep this promise. English law, as said, still denies the third party (*C*) direct contractual rights against *A*, this for some complicated technical reasons into which we need not go. Yet it is no less significant that this legal rule has been continually criticised precisely because it divorces rights from benefits especially where, as here, a person like *C* has a clear benefit in the promise, *C* being the person directly affected by *A*'s breach of it. So to deny *C* any rights, on the basis that only *B*, as the contracting party, has the appropriate 'control' over the right as he alone is in a position to waive it, only repeats but does not justify the highly criticisable legal rule that *C* has no contractual rights. If the law were to change (as in some jurisdictions it already has), *C*, too, would have such a right; he, too, would now have full waivable control over it, if, for example, he did not want the money from *A*. Thus the legal position is far too contingent to support Hart's conceptual point.

There remain one or two other arguments. In a subsequent, slightly revised, version of his theory Hart does allow room for benefit in relation even to criminal or constitutional rights, though this only for such purposes as to describe fundamental freedoms like freedom of speech or of assembly, or to identify the moral considerations that underlie the criminal law against murder, assault and similar wrongs. Here, it is admitted, a benefit-theory can throw light on the interests or needs of an individual which these legal rights are designed to protect; except that Hart at once adds that a benefit-theory would still be 'redundant and even confusing' were it a question simply of explaining the criminal law.[5] But this is a puzzlingly narrow view. Why, we may ask, should an individualistic or moral critic, even if agreeing that there are rights in criminal law which do not go without benefits, still not need to entertain a *general* theory linking right with benefit; why, therefore, should this critic still subscribe to all the criticisms of the benefit-theory? As we have seen, it is precisely a general benefit-theory that can elucidate certain basic features of rights. What would the direct beneficiary of a legal duty be a beneficiary of, if it is not a right? and what would the legal obligation be an obligation for? How, moroever, would we be able to explain why a criminal duty exists, or how far this duty and thereby the right may go? Nor, again, can we dismiss the benefit-theory, as Hart does, on the grounds that, being utilitarian in character, it is more concerned with benefits as a contribution to general utility. In connection with rights the benefit-theory rather puts the emphasis on individual needs or interests. The criminal and constitutional rights earlier referred to all seek personal advantages, usually in the form of personal protection either against other persons or against an autocratic government. This need not exclude utilitarian considerations if, like Mill, we think that only they explain why ultimately we pay attention to moral or just rights at all. But this is quite another matter. For the immediate purpose of analysing rights in terms of its constituents, the element of benefit is not logically capable of being suppressed.

Another situation may cause somewhat greater difficulty. This situation, originally too mentioned by Hart, is one in which a number of persons, conducting a joint and co-operative enterprise, mutually restrict their liberty; those who submit to these restrictions consequently have a right to a similar submission from those who benefit by theirs.[6] While this fully tallies with the benefit-theory, Lyons thinks the following variation does not. The rules of income tax impose a legal duty on everyone to pay tax; if we assume this to be an instance of a joint enterprise with mutual restrictions, one has a moral duty to conform to such a rule just as others have a right to expect that these rules will be observed, that is, that all taxes will be paid. Here, the argument goes, the benefit-theory cannot account for these rights; the legal duties in question, socially useful as they are, create no direct benefits in those having rights. However this argument proves too much. The real reason why one taxpayer has no rights against a defaulting one simply is that the benefit is not personal enough; the defaulter is no doubt guilty of a grave violation of duty, his default may even be grossly unfair to the community at large. The fact remains that the default does not directly affect a particular personal interest; the benefit-theory cannot therefore apply, there being no personal claim against the faulty taxpayer. A law-abiding citizen may of course criticise the defaulter, or denounce him to the authorities, but he does not become the defaulter's personal creditor simply because the tax is not owed to him but to the whole community.[7]

We can now better see benefits connecting with rights as both personal and direct in character, in the sense of constituting an immediate advantage to the person claiming the right. My fellow citizen's duty to pay his income tax or perform his military service certainly might be a benefit to me as a member of the same community, but it is at best an 'indirect' advantage in that it rather benefits the community collectively. This does not mean that social defaulters cannot ever be directly answerable to others, or even confer rights. If a defaulter refuses to be vaccinated against an infectious disease which directly threatens his neighbour, the latter may well advance a personal right against the defaulter endangering him. But this would be so only in circumstances where there are clear and direct risks to an individual's life and limb. Here, indeed, instead of being at most indirect and impersonal, the benefit would again be a very personal one. The benefit-theory thus turns out to be even stronger than is usually thought.

INTERESTS AND RIGHTS

We return more specifically to the notion of interest, though only to deal with its essentials, particularly in its relation to rights, a relation still enmeshed in a great deal of confusion, partly due to the new vogue of the so-called interest-theory about which we later speak. Now it is clear that a right must incorporate an interest just as it must contain a benefit for the right-holder; nonetheless, not every interest gives rise to a right, interest being the wider notion of the two. For, briefly and broadly defined, an interest is simply something one wants or desires, or something one should want or desire. Accordingly, we can distinguish between two meanings of interest, its subjective and its objective sense.[8]

Thus I may have an interest in food because I am hungry, or be interested in a book I want to be instructed by, or in physical exercise which I happen to like. In this subjective sense, I can even be interested in things not at all good or beneficial for me: in drugs and drink, or other acknowledged hazards to health. But this sense, it is quickly seen, gives us little help in relation to rights, for it does not explain whether, or how, rights exist even if we do recognise the interest; the interest only reveals our motives for certain actions, including the reasons for our grievances or the reasons why we seek certain rights. To identify an interest, therefore, only tells half the story, the half in fact we already know, if only because, in this context, we can be supposed fully to know what we desire or want. Not, to be sure, that this interest becomes a useless or dispensable element. We still need a notion of interest if only to show that one cannot have claims, or advance rights, in regard to matters in which one has no possible concern; without a personal interest a claim simply cannot qualify as a right. One cannot have a right, for example, to Darwinian evolution or to the universe having started with a bang. A right, in other words, has to relate to a personal interest for the same reason that it must relate to a personal benefit; without either one could not formulate a personal grievance, or make a personal claim.

What about an interest in a more objective sense? Instead of *having* an interest, something can *be* in one's interest, whether one desires it or not. Bitter medicine is not something one usually wants, although taking it can be eminently beneficial in helping one to get well. Indeed only things objectively beneficial can be in one's interest, a circumstance which excludes many things one might otherwise be interested in. Still, even this objective sense cannot sever all links with desire – it must still allow some room for desiring, or of something being at least potentially desirable. For, if not, the interest instead of emanating from an individual would be a sort of superior imposition, a benefit conferred totally in the absence of personal interest. We should be able to say, Feinberg suggests, that something is in someone's interest because it can be integrated in his total set of desires such that it yields a greater net balance of desire-fulfilment in the long run.[9] Thus if *A*'s major desires are frustrated so long as he is ill, then *A*'s taking unpleasant medicine is in his interest in this desire-related sense. If, by contrast, *A* wants to hang himself, to give him the rope to do it would not be regarded as in his interest; for though getting the rope might be desired subjectively, giving it to him would offend every ordinary notion of doing something for one's objective benefit. To be in one's interest can therefore be interpreted as a presumptive desire for a personal benefit, especially a long-term rather than a short-term, normal rather than unusual, reflective rather than momentary, benefit.

But this, too, does not come anywhere near explaining why any such interest should give rise to rights. Of course a subjective just as an objective diagnostic of interests does tell us why it is we make contracts or seek gifts to acquire rights. Why, for example, we buy, or beg for, rights to food, books or whatever: we do so, obviously, to satisfy immediate interests. Or why we arrange for ways and means to learn a trade, or start an education, or save for a rainy day, obviously all measures to secure for us benefits over time. Yet, again, while this supports the benefit-theory as we explained it before, it does nothing to help with more basic aspects of rights. For one thing, as later chapters will try to make clear, rights created by a contract or gift, what lawyers call rights *in personam*, cannot exist without a framework of more fundamental rights, or rights *in rem*, that is, rights which allow a person both enough freedom of action and enough (proprietary) security over a *res*. For only on the basis of such *in rem* rights can we make contracts or gifts, or acquire advantages or shares in property, thus acquire what lawyers sometimes describe as a 'legal interest' which, too, is an interest resulting from existing legal rights, not the rights from the interest.

For another thing, rights after all are not meant to serve as prescriptions for bitter medicine, nor to tell us what is good or best for us prudentially. Rights, as we have said and shall argue again, are principally designed to give us firm claims against others, especially claims where the interests we have may be resisted by other individuals precisely because of their own interests. To see this better, consider our interest in basic needs. All human beings are interested in food, shelter and clothing, so much so that we do not even have to say that these things are in a person's interest, even less for his benefit; all we say is that he needs food, shelter, and so on, simply in order to survive. As a general rule, nevertheless, all these needs or necessities remain the responsibility of each adult individual to provide for himself; for, as we shall further explain in later pages, it would seriously diminish our individual freedom if we had to provide for others, the great exceptions here being children and, on other grounds, the poor, though neither exception affects the present point. Indeed if everyone's indubitable interest in food automatically created a right, we would arrive at the absurd result that everyone would be relieved of the job of procuring food for himself, since everyone would have a right to have food supplied to him. It follows that however great one's interest in food, this alone cannot *eo ipso* create a right to it.

More important still, we may begin to see that if interests are to be *directly* creative of rights, they have to be viewed not as purely personal benefits or benefits as they relate to one person alone, but viewed as representing wider concerns such as are capable of being commonly shared, that is, shared or sharable as mutually compatible interests, or interests equally applicable to all members of the same group or community. But what are such sharable interests? In general only interests which all of us seek, to enable us to live as free individuals among equal individuals: to live, in other words, in a community which, managing its interpersonal grievances discursively, on the basis of principle, cannot do so unless resorting to certain natural and moral rights. There will be more to say about this.

THE INTEREST-THEORY: A POSTSCRIPT

If the above analysis is correct, what is often called 'the interest-theory' can no longer offer anything like a general theory capable of justifying or explaining the creation of rights, any more than can its once familiar rival known as 'the will-theory'. The interest-theory is to some extent a useful reminder that rights must be interest-related claims, and that thus interest-related, they are profoundly concerned with the benefits or, more broadly with the wellbeing of right-holding individuals. But the theory, in its usual version at any rate, goes significantly further, for it suggests (wrongly, it should now be clear) that rights stem directly from personal interests when, as we have seen, even objective interests do not directly lead to rights, only certain interests do, and then only those which connect with those basic moral considerations generative of natural or moral rights. The will-theory, on the other hand, rather associates rights with the notion of power or capacity, the right-holder being seen as exercising a special ability over the duty-bearer by virtue simply of his ability to make or modify his claim; although even in this respect it is not really clear whether the relevant will or ability is to be one capable of making a claim, in which case the theory would convey little that is new, or whether it is to be an ability capable of imposing a right, in which case however we would be speaking of might, not right.

On a more modest interpretation, it should also be obvious that we in fact need both theories, or more precisely some of the major considerations underlying each, for the proper analysis of a right. We need an interest-theory if only to remind us, as already mentioned, of the interest-relatedness of rights, and we need something of a will-theory as it, too, contains a grain of truth in that it calls attention to the fact that having a right is, either directly or indirectly, to be able to make a claim as well as a claim that is morally or legally answerable, for answerability, as we shall come to see, is what rights are ultimately about. The two theories are then by no means so mutually exclusive as is often thought; too sharp a contrast between them only introduces a false dichotomy. For the will-theory can easily be interpreted as allowing a rightful capacity of making a claim but only under certain conditions, conditions which the interest-theory can be said to supply. However this may be, it is the interest-theory that has recently received renewed prominence, the connection with interests being seen again, yet still no more correctly, as the principal key to rights analysis.[10] Unfortunately this analysis will continue on a wrong course so long as we overlook that interest, like benefit, though constituting an admittedly essential component in rights, still does not and cannot explain why, or under what further conditions, rights can arise at all.

4 Rights and Duties

THE PROBLEM OF CORRELATIVITY

While there are rights with duties and without – 'dutiful' and 'dutiless' rights – it is rights correlative with duties that logically rank as our primary type of rights. It is a distinctive feature of normative rules that they basically operate through pairs of rights and duties, since such rules are concerned not alone with action-guidance but also with the distribution of benefits and burdens as between two individuals. There can be no right, Bentham remarked, unless the duty 'assures' a certain 'good' in the other.[1] What is more, the right-holder does not merely state his interest, however much he does that too, he also claims an appropriate response: that the other should respect his grievance by at least offering a justifying excuse, or by making good an injury he has done, or abstaining from harm he intends to do, or by returning money or a thing which is the claimant's property. Normative relationships, whether moral or legal or both, thus break up into dual components in that two-party relations have to include a right on the one hand with a duty on the other. It would be pointless to say that a person *may* do something without there being other people related to that 'may'; only if there is correlativity can 'may' in fact do its truly distinctive work. Of course the words right and duty are sometimes used in a looser sense, it being said that there can be rights without duties as well as duties without rights. But, as we shall shortly see, whatever may obtain in some cases, our primary logical type remains that of a right with a duty as its correlative.

No other rules are so intimately dependent on right–duty elements. Certainly not technical rules, although they too are action-guiding ('to avoid a chill take a coat'), for they are not rules telling us what we *may* do in relation to others: they only convey what we *can* do, or *how* to do things, designed as they are to be practical answers to specific questions when we happen to be ignorant or uncertain as to what to do in more or less unfamiliar situations. Moral or legal rules must also be distinguished from the rules of games even if the latter also involve two-party (or two-team) relationships. In tennis, it may seem perfectly legitimate to say that one has a 'right' to serve; but what this means is rather that it is one's turn to serve, it being one of the conditions of the game that players serve alternately, to offer each player an equal chance to score points. Unless the chances to display skills are equally, or at least fairly, distributed the whole exercise would not constitute a game as the contest would no longer be an even-handed one. In a game like football a player might well protest that he has a right against being tripped; but this would be an extension of a person's ordinary immunity from assault, an immunity perhaps more urgently watched in games where a contest threatens to become unfair.[2] As far as a game or contest itself is concerned, however, neither side has, strictly speaking, rights just as neither has strictly any duties as neither is bound to continue playing, their activity being entirely voluntary. The players do not stand in a right–duty relationship for another reason as well. Moral or legal rights and duties do allow, as we shall later see, questions as to their respective reasons, which is why we can treat them as *prima facie* or why they can be overridden or qualified. But rules of games cannot accommodate such qualifications precisely because questions of this sort would defeat the whole purpose of the game as they would interrupt, or at least inordinately delay, the very progress of the activity, including its being finalised in due course by one party winning, the other losing. Even games, to be sure, give rise to disputes, but these are normally 'factual' disagreements – whether a ball is 'in' or 'out', did or did not touch the net, and so on; the rules themselves cannot normally be subject to debate.

Since a right is not just a cry in the wilderness but a call for protection, the correlative duty marks out the protective measures to be taken in response. The word right indeed comprises a distinctive public and social element which a word like interest does not similarly project. To say that men have rights and especially basic rights, as to life, limb or property, is to say that a person has a claim to be protected by his community or group against certain evils over which he has no control himself, together with a claim for those (mainly legal) institutions which organise this protection, and this not merely against other persons, but also against governments.[3] To ask for institutional protection is, of course, not to ask for coercion for coercion's sake, it is rather to seek to prevent certain actions as well as to obtain appropriate remedies. Preventive measures would no doubt be preferable to remedial; the trouble is that prevention is not always possible. You cannot prevent all dangerous activities, injuries are bound to occur in spite of rules to the contrary. Protection from dog bites, it has been well remarked, might be secured by prohibiting the keeping of dogs or by destroying all of them. But such radical prohibitions are in practice often impossible, so that we simply have to make do with a state of affairs in which injury will occur, but injury that can be remedied. *Ubi jus ibi remedium* is then another, if somewhat more indirect, way of saying that normative rights and duties are necessarily correlative.

NON-CORRELATIVE DUTIES

Yet it is still frequently asserted that rights and duties are not invariably correlated, that there can be rights without duties as well as duties without rights. Now there admittedly exist certain non-correlative rights and duties, but these turn out to be specific exceptions, of marginal rather than central significance, hence instances which do not really damage our thesis of the primacy of right–duty correlativity.

To look at this first from the viewpoint of duties, take the familiar example of a duty attaching to an office such as an executioner's: the murderer sentenced to be hanged cannot be said to have a right against the executioner, however much the latter remains under a duty to execute the sentence. One reason why there is here no right is that, as earlier mentioned, the murderer has no benefit or interest in being hanged; another and in this place more pertinent reason is that the executioner's duty is not towards the murderer but to the authority which employs him, so that only the latter would have any rights as a principal. Or take what Bentham called 'barren' duties, such as duties of no utility to anyone except a tyrant who, for example, may command his subjects to inform on anyone unfriendly to him. Here, too, one scarcely says that anyone has a 'right' to be denounced; the tyranical duty is a mere imperative addressed to the population at large, not a duty arising from reciprocal interests as between private citizens. In neither case, therefore, is the non-correlativity of the duty logically disturbing.

Another example of a duty without right is a little more complex. This is the well-known duty to be charitable, or to be kind – duties we proclaim in or for situations in which we might think we ought to conduct ourselves in a kind or charitable way, like the boy scout's vow to do at least one good deed every day. To subscribe to a duty of charity or kindness does not obviously create immediate rights. However, the explanation of this is that such a duty is only a way of saying that one 'ought' to be charitable, the 'ought' being a highly general or abstract one: abstract because the duty-bearer cannot benefit all those in need of charity (assuming his means are limited), so that he must still select those among many possible candidates he would wish to benefit, the choice being entirely his. This shows how 'duty' can be used in an extended meaning. Here it is the duty-holder's own sense of duty that is at stake; he can change his mind without becoming answerable to anyone, since others have as yet no concrete grounds to complain that he is not charitable to them in particular. A duty to be charitable is then like a duty to oneself, but a duty which, seen purely as a duty, becomes rather self-contradictory since it conveys that one both must do something and yet may not do it, the duty being entirely within one's own control.[4]

The reason why, in this context, we use the word duty at all is that it now operates as a nominative substitute for deontic verbs such as 'have to', 'must' or 'ought', which have no noun just as the word duty, unlike 'obligation', has no direct verb.[5] So just as some well-wisher may remind you of your 'duty' to take more exercise instead of telling you that you 'must' exercise more for better health, so we can tell ourselves that we 'must' or that it is our 'duty' to pursue particular virtues we happen to prefer. These may well be moral virtues which, in their observance, could make us better people and the world a better place, but they remain, for all that, voluntary undertakings which only last as long as we want them to last; they are not the sort of moral duties which make us responsible to others and in this way bound to them, even when we do not wish to be bound.

This raises another peculiarity: that while we do not normally speak of 'moral duties', we refer to 'moral obligations' often enough.[6] Why should this be? The short answer is that 'duty' and its partner 'obligation' occasionally carry different implications though they mean otherwise largely the same. To have a moral obligation implies that we admit to a moral commitment, either explicitly by making a promise, or more implicitly by accepting a favour or gift, the latter usually with an implied undertaking of reciprocity, at least that of gratitude, with the result that the person to whom I am thus committed has a moral right. By contrast, the word duty, being much broader, usable as it is as a nominative substitute for a self-assumed 'ought' and 'must', does not similarly carry reciprocal commitments; consequently there are no acts or services another can claim from me as of right. The reference to 'duty' in effect merely serves as a sort of reminder that there is a need for charity in the world.

It follows that to argue for duties without rights is then to make a valid as well as, if taken too far, a profoundly invalid point. The valid point is that we do, sometimes, speak of duties in a wider or extended sense whenever we refer to prudential musts, or to personal resolutions, or vows, or precepts of an abstract morality ('always be charitable', 'always be kind'). As this involves us in deontic language, we may speak of 'duties' if we prefer the noun to the corresponding verbs. But this must not lead us away from a central meaning of duty in which it functions as a correlative of right, the duty-holder now being told both that he must do something and that he is critically bound to do it – bound because his deviance from the duty is challengeable not by his own better intentions but by another individual, precisely because that other individual has a right. This meaning obtains where there is a moral or legal rule, or an actual custom or convention, under which what I have to do is expected of me by others just as in similar circumstances I expect it from them.[7] To neglect this correlative sense of duty is to run the risk of obscuring what is most distinctive about a normative two-party relationship.

NON-CORRELATIVE RIGHTS

What of the reverse argument about rights without duties? Here it seems even clearer that rights cannot operate without a correlative, for what would the right now be – a right to or right against — if it did not entail a responsive duty by another individual? Two instances of right which at first sight suggest the contrary are not at all what they seem. Defensive rights, as we saw in Chapter 2, under which a person may do something (like exercising his right of self defence), are rights which, though themselves unaccompanied by any duties or claims against, nevertheless presuppose correlative rights and duties; they presuppose prior normative relationships which 'dutiless' rights can fasten on. Our second instance, somewhat different, is best explained by an example. Suppose a policeman orders you (a motorist) to stop: has he a right to be obeyed? You may of course ask him 'what right have you to stop me?', admitting your duty to stop if the policeman can authenticate his right. Yet even if he does show a right, it is not strictly correlative to your duty, for it is not a right for his own benefit, but rather an authority given to him to maintain public order.

The policeman, like our previous executioner, is acting on behalf of public principals. Indeed only agents, public or private, can be asked to authenticate such rights to act at all. These are rights, we begin to see, which arise in conjunction with an office; they are only rights enabling or entitling one to perform official or public tasks. And so it is with all office-holders who may – and even must – do certain things; their so-called rights thus are more properly 'powers', a concept we further attend to in Chapter 6. At all events, rights thus merging with powers, though furnishing another illustration of the multiple ambiguity of 'may', are not rights that stand in real conflict with our thesis of correlativity.

Still, the thesis of non-correlative rights has been advanced with some energy, in two versions, one moderate, one more extreme. The moderate version does not deny that, typically, rights and duties are 'tightly' correlative. Where *A* owes *B* $10, the right–duty implication is both specific and determinate as *A* now owes what *B* is owed. The mutual implications here are strong, Lyons concedes, because they entail conceptual correlatives: there can be no debtor without a creditor just as there is no right side without a left.[8] But, as Lyons further contends, when we turn from such passive to more active examples this conceptual corelativity loosens considerably; for though rights and duties still denote ordered pairs, the respective contents of these pairs are no longer so matching as before. Suppose *A* is publicly holding forth against his country being at war when he is attacked by some private citizens with more bellicose views. Now, it is thought, *A*'s right to speak has less straightforward correlatives. The duty of other citizens not to interfere is not quite the same as the previous debtor's duty to pay. The debtor must be an identified person, the other citizens can be anyone. Furthermore, *A*'s right to speak derives from his right of free speech, which a legislature (assuming it is bound by relevant constitutional guarantees) can do nothing to abrogate: *A*'s right, it is said, becomes an 'immunity' while the legislature is under a 'disability' to intervene.

Although this argument correctly asserts that the right–duty correlations are tighter with regard to special (or *in personam*) than in relation to general (or *in rem*) rights, and though, as we shall later see, this has various other ramifications especially in relation to rights *in rem*, the fact remains that this does not affect the right–duty correlativity itself. To insist on this is to return to a proposition we have stressed repeatedly: that a right would simply have no normative significance if it did not strive for recognition or protection or did not contain the possibility of a claim against the violator of the right. A right of free speech, as in the above example, thus indicates not only a duty not to interfere with the speaker but extends to anyone, including those who might be angered by what is being said. Nor does the immunity–disability terminology, borrowed from Hohfeld, do anything to disprove the right–duty correlativity, quite apart from the fact (as the following chapter will try to show) that this terminology itself is seriously at fault. For an immunity can be seen as but another way of saying that the speaker has a right not to be obstructed in his free speech, just as the legislature has a corresponding prohibition not to interfere. Again, to turn to another example sometimes given, a right to make a right turn on a red light in California is not a right standing by itself; rather is it a right that specifically introduces an exception to the normal rule, as those coming from the left are now under a duty to give those turning right the right of way.[9]

Yet another argument, especially in connection with free speech, maintains that the fact that one is under a prohibition to intervene still does not imply that another necessarily has a right; for one may still be under a duty not to interfere with the other's activities whether the latter has a right to free speech or not. But this is not really the case. My duty not to interfere with another's free speech is not included in my general duty not to interfere with another's life, limb or speech; the question now is far more specific, namely, whether I can intervene in circumstances where I am unduly angered or even provoked. The question therefore is whether a public speaker has, or should have, an unlimited right to remain unmolested even if his speech causes in others not just bigotry but real distress.[10] Similarly it is misleading to say that an 'active' right such as free speech implies a 'disability' in another, as distinct from a duty. For what can this so-called disability be? As the disability here is not natural or physical but normative, it surely implies a duty to refrain from interfering with free speech, and this quite regardless of whether the correlative is called a right or an immunity.

A more extreme criticism, advanced by Singer, even challenges the view that tight correlations arise in the case of 'passive' rights, as in the relationship of *A* being owed \$10 by *B*.[11] There are, he contends, passive rights where the correlation does not hold. As where *A* promises *B* to pay \$10 to *C* where there is a correlation between *A* and *B*, but *B* has no passive right – this right belongs, if at all, to *C*; or where I have a right to be recognised at a meeting by the chairman, but he is under no corresponding duty to recognise me. Neither example is convincing here. The first, as we suggested in Chapter 3, does not show that the *A–B–C* relationship has to exclude a right–duty correlativity between *A* and *B*, given *B*'s direct benefit or interest in *A*'s promise to *C*. In the second example, my right to speak at the meeting might equally well be regarded as an active right (to speak); yet even disregarding this, my right to be recognised, if as now stated too loosely, easily misses the point that we are now dealing with what is only a conditional right, conditional, that is, upon a number of circumstances (the number of speakers competing, time available, and so on) which it is for the chairman to assess; only if these circumstances go in my favour would the chairman be under a duty to call on me, so that within these limitations, there would be again a right–duty relationship.

Singer advances two further arguments why we cannot imply a right from a duty in some cases at least. One is that we cannot imply this even in relation to 'active' rights such as *A*'s right to collect $10 from *B*. For the fact that *B* has a duty to pay the money does not mean that *A* has himself a right to it; admittedly *A* has such a right if *B* owes *A* the money, but not if *B*'s creditor is *C*, not *A*; it all depends on how the duty arises, on what he calls its 'basis', that is, the antecedent transactions on which the duty rests.[12] But it is difficult to see the relevance of this. If *B* does not owe *A* any money, *A* can have no rights for the simple reason that *B* has no duty: the problem of correlativity does not arise. Furthermore, a 'basis' such as indebtedness or ownership must be presumable if there is to be a right–duty relationship at all. Even where *A*'s right to collect is based on his acting as agent for *C* there is still a right–duty relationship save for this difference that *C*'s place as right-holder is now filled by *A*. Singer's second argument takes us back to the example of free speech. He now says that Lyons has effectively shown that *B*'s prohibition from interfering with *A*'s free speech does not imply that *A* has a right to free speech; for *B* would still be under a prohibition not to interfere with *A*, whether *A* has a right of free speech or not.[13] As already seen, this is not really true. *B*'s duty not to interfere is not just a general but a very specific duty not to interfere with *A*, however provoked *B* may be. If so, it does not seem tenable to maintain, with Singer, that someone may have a right to do something without anyone else having any duties that could be reasonably correlated with that right. What can be maintained is the exact opposite, namely, that once we do have or recognise a right we also acknowledge the necessity for a duty, one capable of giving effect to that right.

All this, it has well been said, is no more than to restore the obvious; for unless rights do imply duties, rights cannot really be understood.[14] What purpose could in any case be served in arguing for rights without duties? Without correlativity, the interests seeking protection would go without it, for there would be no other person whose responsibility would be engaged. A duty, it is true, may not always be very efficacious in its protective effects; it is, nevertheless, the existence of such a duty that makes for the answerability of the claim, its answerability in principle. It goes without saying that the present claims do not refer to grievances for which nobody carries responsibility. If my grievance is that I am not a gifted painter or pianist, this is not something anybody can help. Nor are we speaking about a right to feel pleased, and so on, for these are merely customary forms of vindicating a self-congratulatory attitude where I might otherwise be vulnerable to a charge of conceit or vanity. Our business at present is solely with rights, not about what I, but what others have to do or not to do, hence rights which imply corresponding duties to some action or restraint by others, since without such duties the rights would not be worth stating. In this delimited but utterly crucial sense, rights and duties are then always correlative.

DEGREES OF CORRELATIVITY

The preceding discussion suggests (perhaps it was in fact groping after) some more interesting, if more elusive, points. Correlative as they are, rights and duties are nonetheless only correlative with, so to speak, different degrees of intensity. In some cases, the right–duty relationship is very tight, in others more contingent and so more remote. Tight right–duty correlations arise mainly in personal obligations, a most obvious instance being a debt. Where *D* (debtor) owes *C* (creditor) $10, *D* owes what *C* is owed; *D*'s duty or obligation of indebtedness corresponds to what lawyers call *C*'s right *in personam*. The Roman origin of 'obligation' vividly reveals this close personal bond: in early law, until the debtor repaid what he owed, he remained physically bound to the creditor, virtually like a personal slave. Today, of course, a personal legal obligation only means that one has a right to have or receive money or property from another, though only from him, nobody else. Similar personal rights arise from pledges or promises which latter may comprise positive as well as negative undertakings, that is, they can be promises to do and promises to forbear or abstain. Furthermore, debts or debt-like undertakings are easily treated as transferable assets; specific and enforceable as they are, they turn into bits of wealth that can be bought and sold almost as reified or reifiable commodities. What the law technically describes as 'choses in action' are precisely rights of this sort; not being tangible objects they lie 'in action' rather than 'in possession' as they do not lend themselves to physical custody; but being valuable, often very valuable, they are 'choses' or things such as (to name but a few) a debt, or a share, or an annuity, or dividend, or some pecuniary interest as in a legacy or trust fund; they are assets or benefits which the owner (or transferee) has a right to call in.

Rights *in rem* are of very different character. Unlike rights *in personam* they are not positive or commissive but negative and omissive since their correlative duties inevitably consist of acts of forbearance or non-interference with another's person or property. Thus a right *in rem* to land means everyone has to respect that land by abstaining from trespassing on it, whether deliberately or carelessly. An old legal tradition regards such rights as rights against 'the world' since the person who may break this duty need not be an already identified person but can be anyone in the world capable of committing the trespass. Hence a right against the world does not imply that I have a concrete right against every global inhabitant, only that anybody coming into proximity with me or my property may become a trespasser without his identity being known in advance. And as this eventual trespasser or similar wrongdoer is as yet unidentified, there is for the time being no operative duty attaching to anyone; what there is is merely a contingent, even hypothetical, duty addressing itself to those who by their actions may choose to become trespassers, although the duty will not be operative in the sense of being actionable unless and until a trespass actually occurs. This, however, does not alter the right–duty correlation, at any rate not in principle, since there would be no right *in rem* unless there is a right that can, even if it need not in fact, result in a claim against.

This brings us to another misconception, namely, that the old and canonical division between rights *in personam* and rights *in rem* has to do with two types of rights which, whatever their differences, are logically on a par. Rights *in rem* are not meant to create direct and personal relationships as do rights *in personam*; their purpose is to state claims or rights only against *possible* wrongs. Without rights *in rem*, moreover, we could not even formulate duties which are not purely personal or self-assumed, nor indicate general reciprocal obligations, all of a negative or abstaining kind, yet all of them creative of precisely those aggregate forbearances which alone offer the opportunities for an individual to have or enjoy personal or possessory immunities. Indeed, my right to possessions, like my right to life or limb, not only depend on the duties responding to rights *in rem*, the latter are therefore our basic rights: rights we must have before we can do anything as regards *in personam* rights. As said before, rights *in personam* cannot arise unless we first have rights *in rem*; thus we cannot even have personal rights as creditors or contractors unless we can own the things we wish to sell or exchange; we cannot owe things unless there is somebody who owns them in the first place.

CORRELATIVES AND COMPLEMENTARIES

Rights and duties are correlative in yet another sense, in that they behave as mutual complementaries, each of them making its own distinctive contribution to the two-party relationship. Hence rights and duties are not, so to speak, mirror-reversed reflections of each other. As we shall now see, rights and duties, notwithstanding their correlative correspondence, do not contain the same conceptual elements but perform different tasks, tasks nonetheless closely complementary. A right refers to an individual's interests, while the duty indicates the requisite commissions or omissions protecting those interests. A right reveals a person's complaint or grievance, the duty specifies actions a duty-bearer must avoid. A right defines an area of freedom, the duty specifies conduct for which one is answerable or responsible. Rights, in short, relate to benefits, duties to the burdens responding to these benefits. All of which shows, yet again, why normative (moral like legal) rules, being two-sided affairs, break up into complementary rights and duties: why, more particularly, we have to start with one side's grievance about some action affecting or diminishing his wellbeing physically or materially, whereas on the other side we need to focus on the action itself, how it was done, including whether it was or was not avoidable. Obviously there would be no point making a complaint, let alone a complaint about the gravity of an act, if the other side (the duty-holder to be blamed) could not have helped doing what he did.

With rights and duties now seen as forming a sort of functional complementarity, it becomes easier to observe a concomitant feature, that of the relative primacy of rights. Thus we see, perhaps clearly only now, that questions as to duty are profoundly dependent on questions of right; unless we have rights or answerable grievances, there would be no purpose in investigating what the defendant did, whether his action was or was not avoidable, or voluntary, or deliberate, or merely careless or negligent. This feature, needless to say, runs wholly counter to the well-known thesis of the redundancy of rights. It simply cannot be the case, as the latter thesis maintains, that whether we speak of rights or duties is, at the end of the day, merely a matter of perspective or style since nothing extra is conveyed by using, instead of duty, the language of right.[15] Just as, so this thesis also maintains, corresponding relations like 'being the parent of' or 'being the child of' can easily make do with one half of the correspondence, so 'being a right against' can be satisfactorily rendered by 'having a duty towards'. Hence the word 'right' can be dispensed with, correlated as it is to the notion of duty which adequately describes the two-party relationship, especially in the law. This completely overlooks that rights and duties are inextricably linked precisely because they handle different but conceptually interlocking jobs. Even in natural languages which have no word for 'right' (for example, Greek) this gap is quickly filled, for they can nevertheless be said to have a *concept* of right simply because complementarity implies such a concept, even if it is not actually in use.[16] Without this complementarity, the duty would indeed be 'barren', its accountability due at most to some leviathan, not to fellow human beings with their own concerns and interests since, on this view, it would no longer matter what their rights are.

RIGHT-GENERALITY AND DUTY-SPECIFICITY

There is a further reason for separating rights from duties while nevertheless seeing them as dual components of the same relationship. Rights have a distinctive generality compared with the relative specificity that duties possess; rights are more general being inevitably formulated in broader terms so that they can both direct and, in a way, even survive the corresponding correlative duties meant to protect those rights. A right to life, limb and property, statable as it is in very general language, yet requires, correlatively, a much longer catalogue of duties; for such a right requires a large number of prescriptions or proscriptions if the action-guidance comprised in the duty is to be sufficiently action-specific to be capable of giving effect to the corresponding right. Duties have to be more specific precisely because the duty-holder must be told, not only generally but with some particularity, what he may or may not do, since infringements of the duty can have severe moral or legal consequences, especially if accompanied by punitive ones. This may explain why lawyers often concentrate on duties, whereas moral philosophers appear more preoccupied with rights; but a total inquiry has to deal with both rights and duties, both as correlatives and complementaries.

A distinction between right-generality and duty-specificity dovetails with the different lines in our practical reasoning when it deals with rights and duties respectively. Our reasoning about rights is about principles, particularly the reasons that support the freedoms or benefits we seek as individuals among individuals. On this level of generality we reason about rights not in a doctrinally fixed but in a *prima facie* way, that is, as qualifiable or overridable, though not (and this is a crucial point) as directly overrulable rights. If rights were indeed constantly overrulable we would in effect abandon the requirement of treating like cases alike; coherent reasoning about rights would become impossible since we would no longer have any rule or principle in terms of which the same or similar rights could in fact be treated the same or similarly. This does not at all detract from their *prima facie*-ness, for it is one thing to be firm about settled rights, quite another thing to be kind to exceptions if and where new circumstances arise. Our practical reasoning about rights then is often reasoning about their possible qualifications if and where weightier considerations come to the fore.

This idea of *prima facie* rights stems of course from the notion of *prima facie* duties introduced by Ross.[17] Ross, seemingly, wished to make two points at once. On the one hand, he wished to identify a category of duties which were not absolute; a duty to keep a promise, for example, might be overridden for a superior moral reason such as to prevent mischief by the promisee; and a promisor might accordingly break his promise by refusing to give a gun to someone about to commit murder. On the other hand, he wished to stress that while we can break a duty where new facts occur (as they frequently do occur) we break a duty only with compunction, as we somehow remain under the residual spell of the strength of the duty we originally recognised. Ross's notions are not free from difficulty. If, one criticism goes, his *prima facie* duty is merely there to be cancelled, however reluctantly, why call it a duty; for if the duty is vacated, the *prima facie* duty disappears, and if not vacated the duty remains absolute.[18] This objection seems perhaps a little insensitive to the idea of '*prima facie*-ness' which merely seeks to indicate the selective qualifiability of normative rules; a feature which may not even be great news since even natural rights have never been regarded as absolutely unqualifiable, even in their heyday in the eighteenth century.[19]

Another and more serious difficulty is that Ross's *prima facie* duty does not satisfactorily cope with what he saw as our intuitive ambivalence about breaking a duty such as that of keeping promises. For reflection shows that the ambivalence now arises not so much because the duty, being only *prima facie*, is liable to be overridden, but rather because we are faced with a conflict which has its real source in the primary conflict between two rights. In our previous example, there is precisely such a conflict between the potential murderer's right to his weapon and the potential victim's right to life which latter right would be dangerously threatened were the promisor to hand back the gun; the promisor's ambivalence therefore originates in a conflict between these two rights held by others, not because of a tension in the duty itself. Not only does this again confirm the primacy of rights, it also suggests that the notion of *prima facie*-ness, with its attendant idea of 'open' generality, is particularly applicable to rights, while duties are better kept to their own domain as right-responsive complementaries.

This approach may also have the advantage of lending sharper focus to features that pertain to duties especially. As we saw, our inquiry with regard to duties turns mainly on this: whether an injurious action is or is not avoidable, this being the action for which the duty-holder is to be responsible. The purpose of this inquiry, very broadly, is to determine whether, in the words of the well-known adage, the duty-holder's 'ought implies can': whether, that is, he *could* not have done what he ought not to have done. Obviously a person cannot be responsible unless he acts voluntarily and not due to outside causes, or causes over which he has neither conscious nor any known control. Accordingly 'can' means that the duty-holder has the capacity as well as the motivation to do what he did. His capacity, very briefly, will have to be judged by what in our common knowledge human beings are typically capable of, and his motivation by what he in fact intended to do: so if *A* hates *B* and wants to kill him some time in the future, the fact that *A* kills him negligently today is not doing an act for the purpose of murder, even if the negligence is due to *A*'s hatred for *B*.[20] This, indeed, illustrates once again how action-specific duties are, just as it shows how this action-specificity raises profoundly empirical questions, quite unlike questions relating to rights which are questions which rather pertain to basic or overriding moral principles.

5 A Hohfeldian Digression

HOHFELD'S BASIC SCHEME

Any analysis of rights must take some account of Hohfeld's contribution, perhaps the most influential of its kind, in fact recently described as 'a paradigm of philosophy'.[1] Hohfeld was certainly not the first to recognise 'right' as a very ambiguous word, but his was the first attempt to sort out its meanings systematically.[2] Arranging rights according to their various correlatives and opposites, he divided them into two squares: one based on claims and liberties, the other comprising powers and immunities. In briefly reconsidering these divisions, we do so not to survey Hohfeld's work as a whole, but with the object of re-examining, as it happens very critically, his three central themes: (a) his distinction between claims and liberties, (b) his views of the 'no-right', as he called a liberty's correlative, and (c) his views of powers and immunities.

For Hohfeld the most important distinction is undoubtedly that between 'rights' strictly so-called, what he also calls claim-rights, and 'privileges' which the literature now usually refers to as liberty-rights, or more briefly liberties, a variation we have already followed and shall continue to follow, since this has the advantage of booking 'privilege' for a more specialised usage the next chapter will further specify. Now rights and liberties are distinguished because they are rights with different correlatives and opposites. The correlative of a strict right, or claim-right, is of course a duty, in that if *X* has a right against *Y* that, for example he (*Y*) stay off his land, *Y* is correlatively under a duty so to stay off; *Y*'s duty to stay off here being the converse equivalent of *X*'s right to the same. For Hohfeld, *X*'s right is but one phase of the total relation between *X* and *Y*, *Y*'s duty being but another aspect of the same relation. So if it is true that *X* has a right against *Y*, then it is also true that *Y* has a duty toward *X*.[3]

In the case of a liberty, the respective incidents are different. Instead of asserting a right in *X* together with a duty in *Y*, we rather assert, Hohfeld thinks, that *X* has a right to do *p* in the sense of *X* having a liberty to do what he is doing without *X* having any corresponding claims against *Y* since *Y* is under no correlative duty toward *X*. The only correlative in *Y* is that he himself has no right to claim that *X* abstain from doing *p*, a correlative which Hohfeld describes, perhaps for want of a better word, as a no-right.[4] That is, *Y* has a no-right that *X* stay off his (*Y*'s) land, while *X* has the liberty of not staying off that land. A liberty thus is the negation of any duty (for *X*) to stay off, while the no-right is the opposite of any right that *Y* may have against *X*. If, in short, the correlative of right is duty, and of liberty no-right, right is negated by no-right, duty by liberty. So we arrive at the well-known diagram of Hohfeld's in which the jural correlatives are placed horizontally to each other, and the jural opposites or contradictions vertically:

Right	Duty
No-Right	Liberty

According to Hohfeld, as well as other Hohfeldians, the main value of distinguishing rights from liberties is to avoid possible confusion in our legal as sometimes also in our moral reasoning, since we are liable, it is thought, to reason to conclusions which are justified in terms of liberties but not of rights. This sort of confusion, it is further contended, is particularly evident in situations of conflicting rights such as often occur in industrial disputes. In one well-known case,[5] the plaintiff, having had a dispute with a trade union and union officials after refusing to discharge certain workmen not members of the union, the union officials, to exert greater pressure, compelled the plaintiff's main customer to cease to deal with him, by threatening to call out that customer's workmen as well. The defendant officials were held liable in damages for the loss to the plaintiff caused by the withdrawal of his customer. The defendants, the court said, acted illegitimately against the plaintiff. The latter, like every citizen, had a right or liberty (terms the court here used interchangeably) to pursue his business in his own way, unless in so doing he infringed the rights of others. The plaintiff's right was to deal with other persons willing to deal with him, the question therefore being whether the strikers had interfered with this right.

Hohfeld's view was that the court here confused the plaintiff's liberty with his right to carry on business; the court committed a *non sequitur* in concluding that because the plaintiff undoubtedly had a liberty to pursue his business, he therefore had a right to pursue it; the fallacy was to transform a liberty, the correlative of which was only a no-right, into a right with a corresponding duty not to interfere. But, looking again, there was in fact no such fallacy. The court was not at all concerned with liberties whose correlatives are no-rights, but with liberties *alias* rights whose correlatives are duties. What purpose would have been served to identify a no-right rather than a duty? The question was whether the union officials had or had not broken a duty by doing something injurious: to find a no-right would not have helped at all, since a no-right, as Hohfeld himself explains, negates a duty, it does not affirm or establish one. In speaking of a liberty, moreover, the court did not refer to a liberty in Hohfeld's (privilege) sense, but to a liberty in a wider sense of right, a sense which persuasively supported the plaintiff's right to carry on his business without interference while it weakened the union's case that their interference was in the circumstances justifiable or excusable.

This was, then, the sort of case in which any question of a liberty arose not on behalf of the plaintiff, but of the defendant; for the real question was whether the plaintiff's right against injurious interference could nonetheless be construed as qualified by the union's own liberty, indeed liberty now taken in a strict or defensive sense, to pursue its own interests, although in the event the union was held to have no such defence as its officials were thought to have exceeded a legitimate manner of pursuing these interests, their tactics being regarded as unduly intimidatory. This case, like several similar ones, can therefore be seen as not at all involving a logical mistake. The present difficulty rather is one of weighing the moral reasons or, more broadly, the 'policy' most apt to adjust the parties' opposing interests. In all these cases of directly conflicting or colliding rights, the dispute is thus not resolved by appealing to a distinction between rights and liberties, or between assertive and defensive rights. Or, putting this in another way, in all these cases the question of whether one has an assertive right exactly coincides with the question of whether the other has a defensive right. For the precise issue comes down to this: of determining the extent of a right to non-interference, given the fact that the other side does have some right to interfere. In fact, the issue ultimately remains the same whether the question is presented as one of delimiting an assertive right, or a defensive right, or a combination of both.[6]

RIGHTS, LIBERTIES AND NO-RIGHTS

Hohfeld's right–liberty distinction is flawed in another respect.

Though he rightly distinguished rights from liberties, he thought rights and liberties to be, so to speak, rivals, thereby overlooking that they perform divergent roles. His views are perhaps best understood through an example he much discussed. If *X* buys himself a shrimp salad, he has a right to that salad, although he may get the colic eating it; hence all those who, unlike him, have not bought this salad or have no comparable right to it, have a duty not to interfere with his shrimp salad, whether he eventually eats it or not. Hohfeld sees this situation as also giving rise to a liberty on the part of *X*, the salad buyer; he has a liberty against *Y*, *Z* and all others as to eating the salad, while *Y*, *Z* and so on have no-rights that X should not eat the salad.[7]

This last differentiation seems both redundant and vacuous as it adds nothing that makes a normative difference. If I have a right of non-interference against you in respect of my shrimp salad, my so-called liberty to eat the salad, as well as your no-right to interfere with it, is already implied by my right against you not to interfere. The no-right therefore conveys nothing new; for my right includes my choice to eat or not to eat the salad, either choice being protected by the corresponding duty not to interfere. Nor is another example of Hohfeld's of greater assistance. Suppose, he suggests, the owner (*X*) contracts with *Y* that he will never eat this particular salad, but makes no such contract with *Z*. Now, Hohfeld says, *X*'s relations with *Y* and *Z* are 'fundamentally different', since as regards *Y*, *X* has no liberty of eating the salad, yet he has a liberty with regard to *Z*.[8] But, again, this is a misleading point. As regards *Y*, it is true, *X* has no right to eat the salad, having sold this right to *Y*, who therefore can stop or penalise him by a contractual action. As regards *Z*, on the other hand, *X* has every right, not just a liberty; for *Z* is not only under a no-right with regard to *X*'s salad, he is under a duty not to interfere both with *X*'s salad and with *X*'s eating it.

Yet another example shows how far Hohfeld was from fully appreciating the nature of a liberty or liberty-right, especially if we regard this as being, as we have argued, an essentially defensive right. Suppose *X*, the owner, tells *Y*: 'I give you the liberty to try to eat the shrimp salad, but I do not promise not to interfere with you'. Here, maintains Hohfeld, *Y* has a liberty at least to the extent of not violating any rights of *X*'s if *Y* does succeed in eating the shrimps; but *Y* has no rights, nor has *X* any duties *vis-à-vis* *Y*. This example, too, can be explained quite differently. Since *X* gives *Y* a permission to eat the salad, withdrawable though that permission be, *Y* has a clear right to eat the salad so long as the permission is not withdrawn. We can say

Y now has a right or liberty since the permission gives him a defence. It is not strictly wrong to say that *X* has a no-right that *Y* not eat the salad, but it seems somewhat pointless to say this, particularly after *X* gave *Y* a permission to eat it while he could. This permission, admittedly, *X* can withdraw at any time so as to terminate further eating by *Y*, but *Y may* for the time being eat it, thus has a right to eat it – the more so since *X* cannot force *Y* to disgorge morsels which *Y* has already in his mouth. Once we see the liberty or permission as a defensive right (defensive because the right-holder is not making any affirmative claims, or claims against, merely exercising a liberty or permission now available to him), what really matters is not whether there is a no-right on the other side but whether, or to what extent, *Y*'s defence does hold.

This leads to another point. The exact co-relation, as has been often remarked, is in any case not between liberty and no-right, but either between a liberty-not and a no-right, or a liberty and no-right-not. If *Y* has a liberty to walk on *X*'s grass, *X* has a no-right that *Y* should not walk on it, and *X* has a no-right that *Y* should pay $10 if *Y* has a liberty-not to pay that money. This rectification certainly puts the no-right in its more correct place: now to ask what a no-right is immediately allows the answer that it is the negation of a right or claim-right, just as the negation of a duty is obviously a no-duty, now described as a liberty-not. Still, even though this correction is, formally, perfectly in order, it still does not make the no-right normatively or deontically more informative: *X*, in our previous examples, can do nothing with that no-right so long as *Y*'s defence or liberty holds. Indeed to say that *X* has a no-right with regard to *Y*'s walking on his grass tends to obscure the much more interesting fact that to the extent that *Y*'s right so to walk holds, *X* is under a duty not to interfere with *Y*. To see this better take the following statement by *X* to *Y*: 'You have no right to beat this child.' The full force of his surely implies that *Y* has a duty not to beat it; not a duty, to be sure, amounting to a general prohibition of beating the child, only a duty not to beat this particular child in the particular circumstances envisaged here. In other words, the deontic significance of negating a right is to imply a duty or, rather, a duty-not.

Unless this connection is made, Hohfeld's no-right does not seem very helpful in any talk focusing on rights, even if it is not technically wrong for purely logical (negatory) purposes. This, too, may explain many of the radical criticisms of Hohfeld by later theorists: that the no-right represents nothing; or can represent a white elephant; or represents no more than a desire for symmetry, for Hohfeld could not have his square without the no-right; or if it represents anything this is merely the negative side of a claim-right, yet another illustration, well known in the history of thought, of taking what we deny as real in itself.[9] Also, those on the other side who regard the no-right as something that does have legal or normative significance do not really explain what this special significance is. Even Hohfeld, when challenged that liberty-no-right does not constitute a distinctive jural relation, could only call this a misunderstanding which overlooks that a rule of law that *permits* is just as real as a rule of law that *forbids*.[10] But just this will not do, unless we also say that to permit you to walk over my land not only gives you a right to walk over it but also puts me under a duty not to interfere so long as the permission lasts.

THE DUTY–LIBERTY RELATION

We have seen that Hohfeld presents duty and liberty as mutual opposites. As Hohfeld's square shows, if *A* is under a duty to *B* to do *X*, he (*A*) is not under a liberty; and if *A* is under a liberty to do *X*, he is not under a duty. So stated, this contrast is wrong, since duty and liberty do not exclude but rather imply each other. Duty and liberty, far from opposites, are closely related: 'must', we can say, implies 'may'. So, to take Hohfeld's own example, if someone is under a contract to do work on another's land, he has both a liberty and a duty to enter that land.[11] The statements '*A* is duty-bound to do *x*' and '*A* is at liberty to do *x*' can both be true. Certainly the two are opposites if the contrast is between a duty to do and a liberty not to do, but there is no logical opposition if the contrast is between a duty and a liberty *simpliciter*. Hohfeld must have realised this, for, though his square does not show this awareness he did say that a liberty negates a duty if the liberty we speak of has a content or tenor precisely opposite to that of the duty in question. So seen negation does hold, for to negate a duty now results in a liberty-not, while the logical opposite of a liberty is a prohibition or duty-not. So the denial of a duty to pay tax amounts to a liberty not to pay it, and the denial of the prohibition to walk on another's land turns into a liberty so to walk.

What, more interestingly, emerges is however this: that, with our logical contrasts now more fully restated, we get two pairs of four concepts, which four concepts – as Fitch has shown – can be presented in the square of opposition of traditional logic.[12] The first pair, comprising duty, liberty, prohibition (duty-not) and exemption (liberty-not) then becomes:

	Subalterns:	*Subalterns:*
Contraries:	Duty	Prohibition
Sub-contraries:	Liberty	Exemption

In this square, it wil be noticed, only the notions diagonally opposite each other are contradictories, in that a duty negates an exemption, and a prohibition a liberty. The notions appearing vertically to each other are subalterns, which is to say (as already noticed) that a duty implies a liberty, and a prohibition an exemption. The concepts horizontal to each other are contraries and sub-contraries, respectively, that is, duty and prohibition are contraries, liberty and exemption sub-contraries. The point of this is, of course, that contraries as distinct from contradictories cannot both be true, so that duty and prohibition cannot both relate to the same person in the same respect, whereas sub-contraries cannot both be false, and hence liberty and exemption cannot both fail to relate to the same person to the same action. Thus while it cannot be true that *A* is both under a duty and a prohibition of walking on *B*'s grass, it cannot be false that *A* has a liberty of walking on *B*'s grass as well as an exemption from walking on it.

Furthermore, since a right is the converse equivalent of a duty, one can place the right together with its contraries, sub-contraries and subalterns in a corresponding square of opposition. So starting with the right as the correlative of duty, the correlative of prohibition would be a right-not, that of exemption a no-right and that of a liberty a no-right-not. If, as in our previous example, *X* has a liberty to walk on *Y*'s grass, then *Y* has no right, or a no-right, that *X* should not walk on his grass. The traditional square, in which the contraries and sub-contraries are again horizontal to each other, and the subalterns vertical, then arranges itself as follows:

Right	Right-not
No-Right-not	No-Right

According to Fitch, to whom we owe these diagrams, the term 'no-right', introduced by Hohfeld, and the terms 'right-not' and no-right-not', introduced here, though obviously artificial, are nevertheless indispensable since our language provides no other appropriate words, rather relying on the passive voice to handle converse notions as those above.[13] But this is not altogether so. For one thing, one may doubt whether the terms right-not and no-right-not are in fact indispensable, if only because their permissive modalities are already contained in the more basic 'right' or 'no-right'. As we earlier saw, to have a right is already to have a right-not: the right to walk also gives a right not to walk (not as regards all rights, admittedly, inalienable rights now being excluded, though as regards these the question does not arise); hence in this respect the logic of 'may' seems to differ from that of 'must'. However this may be, the notion of 'right-not' is in fact adequately provided for, this by the word 'immunity' which seems linguistically to be our most natural correlative of prohibition. Hohfeld, it is true, wants to accommodate immunities in a separate scheme, but (to anticipate a little) he was apparently only led to adopt this approach because his basic scheme was too narrow, allowing as it does only for contradictories, but not contraries.

The traditional squares of opposition also have a more unexpected advantage in that they show, albeit more implicitly than explicitly, a point to which we have called repeated attention, namely, that correlative rights and duties have a logical priority or pre-eminence over other rights, whether defensive rights or liberties, or whether rights more akin to powers. Only because we have such basic or prior rights do we have the other sorts of rights, secondary or dependent in their nature as these now, even more clearly, turn out to be. This important point, too, becomes a casualty in Hohfeld's scheme.

POWER AND LIABILITY

Hohfeld saw power and its cognates as belonging to a logically different set of right-related concepts, and he devised the following diagram in which correlatives stand horizontally and opposites vertically to each other:

Power	Immunity
Disability	Liability

Now Hohfeld considered these as very different from rights and liberties. Different, first, because the correlative of a power is a liability, its negation or opposite a disability; different, secondly, because powers have to do not with basic relations, like rights, but with changes in those relations, that is, changes in legal relations brought about, not by natural facts such as death or incapacity, but by a person with superior control in that he has the (legal) power to effect a particular legal change.[14] Hohfeld here argues mainly through examples, some of which raise more questions than they resolve. One example of a power is of *A* abandoning his thing, so enabling another to appropriate it; another is of *A* selling or transferring his property to another, or of making a gift of it; yet another example is of *A* making an offer of a contract to *B*, thus giving *B* a power to accept while putting himself (*A*) under a corresponding liability to be subjected to a decision (an acceptance) the offeree might make.

Although Hohfeld regards 'right' as an 'unfortunate' and 'loose' term for these as for other instances, it is nevertheless difficult to see why an owner cannot be said to have a right to abandon his thing, or sell it, or give it away. If it is objected that a right to dispose of one's things has no specific corresponding duty, this objection would be a mistake. The simple reason is that a right of disposition, a general *jus disponendi*, is implied in the right of property, the proprietor having a right *in rem* against interference whatever he does with his own *res*, in his own interest. It is quite possible, of course, to have or control important property merely by having a *jus utendi* without a *jus disponendi*: land or houses, for example, can be very profitably enjoyed without any right of selling them. But this is not really the present meaning of a property right which does not dissociate a right of user from a right to dispose; even if the proprietor did lack a right to sell, this would rather mean that others would be under no duty not to intervene should the former theaten to sell. Similarly with regard to another of Hohfeld's examples, that of a landlord re-entering for a condition broken, where the tenant, by breaking his agreement, terminates the tenancy and therewith his own right of possession or quiet enjoyment, reviving the landlord's basic or residual proprietary right of regaining or reclaiming what is his. The landlord here does not merely exercise a power, but his right or his right of re-entry as it is technically called, and he may exercise this latter right because of his residual right of property. To give notice, to foreclose or to resume property, or to terminate a contract generally, are simply instances of defensive rights, rights discussed in Chapter 2.

Neither is it very clear why the power-holder should be credited with a 'volitional control' now declared to be 'paramount'. The owner does not 'paramountly' change legal relations by any of his aforementioned acts; if he sells his property to me, he changes his legal status as much as in buying I change mine. We both change it by mutual consent, so that it is difficult to see what new element the word 'change' here conveys. If you change your legal position *vis-à-vis* me by your selling and my buying *x*, then you perhaps also change your legal position merely by consuming or destroying *x* — you are no longer *x*'s proprietor *vis-à-vis* the world since *x* no longer exists. What is more, any such change of legal relations is in any case not peculiar to powers, but is involved in the exercise of all rights. Wherever I insist on my right to property or my right to non-interference I change the relations between the duty-holder and myself, just as where I exercise my (defensive) right of criticism or fair comment and so alter the other's legal position *vis-à-vis* me, for the other is now worse off as his reputation may be blemished without his having any remedy for this loss. Nor, again, does a person in accepting the offer of a contract 'impose' his will on the offeror; indeed, it is not at all illuminating to see the offeree as having a power that puts the offeror under a liability, if only because the so-called power, if exercised, makes the offeree as 'liable' as the offeror. And if, on the contrary, we suppose that no offer is made, are we then supposed to say, as Hohfeld's terminology would indeed invite us to, that the offeree's 'power' is negated, giving him now a 'disability' while the offeror now has its correlative, that is, an 'immunity'?

This is not all. If the power–liability relation is to be so broadly viewed, to cover any change of legal relation, obvious absurdities result. So if 'legal change' is to include the making of gifts, the potential donees, as Hohfeld himself admitted, come under a 'pleasant' rather than an 'onerous' liability.[15] Except that the beneficiaries still remain free to reject the gift, which however does not say much for their alleged 'liability'. Does a testator's 'power' to bequeath his property entail the correlative that the heir is under a 'liability' to him? Even if the inheritance is highly desired by their heir, can this be a liability in any sense? And since everybody can be made to inherit, does every possible person come under a 'liability' to have an advantage thrust on him? Worse still, Hohfeld's power–liability relation can equally well apply to delictual as to the above contractual or 'transactional' acts. For just as I have a power to change your legal position by lending you money, so I can have a power to change your and my legal position by inflicting an injury: the injured party, having before a no-right against me, now has a right for compensation. Indeed, even in situations in which an action is prohibited – as delictual actions of course are – there would be a change in the parties' legal relation since one party could now be said to have a 'power' to inflict a tort, while the other would be under a 'liability' to receive it.[16]

Fortunately Hohfeld's other examples are not quite so vulnerable. A trustee certainly can be said to have a power to sell or manage another's estate. An agent, though normally expected to act within his scope of authority, yet may sometimes have a power to submit his principal to contractual liability to a third party, notwithstanding his principal's instructions to the contrary. And a legislature may have the power to declare, by statute, that all those between sixteen and sixty are liable to serve as jurors.[17] The immediate question is why we allow the term 'power' in such cases but not in the examples mentioned before. The short answer is that we are now dealing with persons who wield certain capacities in relation to others, in the sense that they have rights over others' persons or property. A trustee may manage, according to his own discretion, property not his own; an agent, though similarly under an obligation to act prudently and faithfully in the interests of his principal, can in some cases, nevertheless, make the latter liable against his consent; and a legislature may impose upon us certain liabilities, it being assumed that the legislature as the supreme law-making authority may issue laws which we as citizens are under an obligation to obey, whether any such law bids us to serve as jurors, or to serve in the army, or pay our taxes, or whatever other act legislators vote to make compulsory. In these cases, the specified powers define the various offices; that of the trustee, or contractual agent, or that of a legislature in an organised society. Furthermore, holding such offices, the power-holders can even be said to possess certain capacities of volitional control, for it is precisely the function of these offices that they do have specified areas of control. The fact remains that even if such power-holders *may* do certain things with regard to others, they are quite unlike ordinary right-holders; unlike because they are also charged with appropriate duties, in particular the duty to see to it that the rights they have are exercised properly and in good faith. Powers, as we shall later see in greater detail, are then amalgams of rights and duties peculiar to specific offices; they no longer even fit into the particular scheme which Hohfeld devised.

IMMUNITY AND DISABILITY

If the above analysis is correct we also no longer require a separate schema for immunities and disabilities. For if the term 'power' can and, as we shall see, must be given a different meaning from that Hohfeld suggests, then 'immunity', too, becomes highly suspect if seen as the logical opposite of power or as the correlative of disability. This collapse, to be sure, does not leave the immunity unaccounted for, since, as we have earlier remarked, the immunity coincides with the right-not, or at least largely so coincides for it retains a special meaning in connection with 'privilege' as we shall further notice in Chapter 6. For the present, however, the upshot is that to say a person has an immunity from arrest is merely to say that he has a right not to be arrested.

The correlative of this immunity or right-not is thus not a disability but simply a prohibition. As a result the disability turns out as a term with no particular work to do, not at all surprisingly when we reconsider the word. 'Disability' is ambiguous, for it can be factual or normative. If factual, it is the opposite of ability: an able man can do what a disabled man cannot; to say that a man suffers from a disability is to report a (disabling) fact about him. And if 'disability' is considered normatively, it means that I *may* not do a specified act because of some legal or moral restriction; to suffer a disability thus becomes a duty not to do what I otherwise could do. So that, again, once we leave the factual for the normative realm, the word disability is immediately coupled with that of duty, or more exactly with that of prohibition or duty-not. In this light the word disability seems highly expendable; normatively it can indeed be given up without qualms.

6 Permission, Power and Privilege

OTHER RIGHTS: PERMISSIONS

Apart from our two basic sorts of rights, the right strictly so-called and the defensive right or liberty or liberty-right we earlier identified, there exist various other right-like notions such as the permission, or power, or privilege, the true nature of which needs to be further explored if we are to understand how right-related these notions are.

To begin with permissions, let us first put aside an aspect of no present concern, that is, the situation where a legal system not having prohibited a particular act, the question arises as to whether this lack of prohibition entails a permission (sometimes called a 'weak' permission) to do the act – a matter on which views greatly differ, mostly depending upon whether the legal system is regarded as 'open' or 'closed'.[1] The more interesting question at present is what, to put it a little crudely, a permission actually permits. One feature that needs bringing out immediately is that a permission to play (for example) implies that we may either play or not play, the permission giving us a complete option to do as we wish. A permission is therefore the same as some rights but is wider than other rights, for while some rights also give us a full option either to do nor not to do, other rights, those known as inalienable, give us only an entitlement to do without an option not to do. This may be the reason why we naturally speak of our rights to life, limb or liberty but never of our permissions to any of these things: a 'permission' to life or limb does not make very much sense.

Such a permission does not make real sense for another reason as well. To say that a person has a right to life, and so on, is to state something about that person himself; however, to say that a person has a permission rather conveys that his permissive capacity derives from somebody else, from a person who has the right to give or grant that permission. This assumes that the person permitting has himself a sufficient right out of which he can, so to speak, carve out a right for the 'permittee'. Yet even assuming a permission must come from another person, the permission so given normally amounts to a defensive right: so if *A* is permitted by *B*, the owner, to walk on *B*'s land, *A* cannot claim to (be permitted to) walk on that land as if he had an assertive right, the reason being that in permitting *A* so to walk, *B* merely tolerates *A*'s walking over his (*B*'s) land; for example, permits him to do so for a stated time or specified purpose, a permission which thus reserves its unilateral revocability by the 'permittor'. Indeed many, if not most, permissions are essentially 'tolerations' of this sort.[2] This does not mean that *B* can withdraw his permissions at any point. If I license another to eat my meat or to burn my wood, says an old legal case, I can withdraw this licence at any time, but not after the meat is eaten or the wood burnt, for then my property is either altered or destroyed.[3] Similarly *A*'s permission to walk over *B*'s grass cannot be completely arbitrarily revoked, for *A* cannot be left stranded in the middle of *B*'s lawn; *A* must still have the right to return or to complete his walk.

So for *A* to be given a permission to walk on *B*'s land is to allow him, in effect, three sorts of things. On the one hand, *A* may walk on *B*'s land, or not walk, as *A* prefers; in which case *A* has at least a (defensive) liberty in that he is free to intrude upon *B*'s land inasmuch as he is no longer under a duty to abstain from trespassing. On the other hand, *A* is only free to walk because his permission comes, expressly or implicitly, from a person whose interest is not only directly affected by the permitted act but is an interest that relates to the permittor's own person or things, in respect of which only he can give a permission at all. Thirdly, the permission is always terminable by the permittor except that the permittee cannot be left in a changed position unduly detrimental to him. This third condition shows a permittee's right to be a little different from some of the other defensive rights we discussed in Chapter 2. There we saw such rights as the right of fair comment or self-defence to be based on their own moral reasons, reasons providing independent support for the right; here the defensive right is given by the proprietor himself, in that he consents to another's using or abusing his own property. Rather more so than a defensive right or liberty, a permission then represents a clear application of the principle of *volenti non fit injuria*; having given his consent, the permittor can no longer complain of an injury covered by his consent, except that he remains free to revoke his permission, subject to the condition that the permittee does not remain stranded or in a worse position as a result only of having engaged in the permitted act.

The former permissions should not be confused with permissions which are intended to constitute full rights, rights not to be revocable at will; such permissions can also give *A* an assertive claim to walk on *B*'s lawn, whether he is already on that lawn or not. Such permissions are commonly based on a proper legal transaction whereby a licensee buys or acquires, for a price, the advantages he seeks from the licensor. Here the permission amounts to a full contractual entitlement as between *A* and *B*; a contractual right which sometimes may even ripen into a right *in rem*, as do, for example, rights of easement or servitude. That is, the contractual rights created between *A* and *B* will attach as benefits or burdens to their respective pieces of land and so enure to their successors after them; contractual permissions, licences or rights so ripen into proprietary incidents, though for this to happen various strict conditions have to be satisfied.[4] As these sorts of arrangements become irrevocable, we no longer talk of permissions simply because 'irrevocable permissions' does not convey anything distinctive; terms as 'valid grant' or 'contract' or, for that matter, 'right' already imply that the original permission has long since ceased to be freely revocable. Something similar can be said of a second type of more permanent permission which arises by way of appointment: where *X* appoints *Y* as his trustee or executor, *Y* obtains a 'power' to act for *X*. Here, too, it is no longer useful to speak of a permission since the trustee cannot be removed from his office, at least so long as he acts satisfactorily. However where *X* appoints *Y* to act for him merely as his agent whose mandate can be more freely withdrawn, we might well speak of the agent's permission but still prefer to talk of his 'power' or 'authority' as an agent, the reason being that the latter terms, which include a permission anyhow, do not make the agent's powers less revocable. The result is that when we speak of permissions we typically have wholly revocable permissions in mind, that is, permissions that do not amount to assertive rights, only to defensive liberties.

THE NOTION OF POWER

In re-examining the nature of a power we shall again not be concerned with various uses of 'power' which do not impinge on our theme – uses which refer to 'normative powers', or 'power-conferring rules', or 'facilities' that enable us to engage in certain things such as contracts and so on; indeed, uses rather intended to expose the shortcomings of an imperativist theory of law.[5] Neither shall we here be concerned with the old association of the word 'power' with rights, the latter having often been defined in terms of powers or capacities, mainly as part of the so-called will-theory of rights (already considered in Chapter 3) – a usage now anyhow abandoned for the simple reason that one can have a right without any appropriate power or capacity. So if one speaks of a power over another this would be only a power due to, and informed by, the right: it is the right that explains the power, not the power the right.[6]

Our business, accordingly, is solely with the problem of how, or why, a power can constitute another sort of right, particularly when we refer to such powers as a policeman's power of arrest or a trustee's power of sale. These power-holders, and others like them, undoubtedly have some right: the only question is what sort it is. Obviously a power is more than a permission, even if both allow that one person may do things in relation to another person or his property. It is more, for one thing, because the power is usually meant to be something of a lasting permission, to endure as long as the power-holder's task remains to be done. For another and more important thing, a power can be seen to involve both rights and duties as these jointly attach to certain tasks or offices. The true logical secret of a power, so our argument will now be, is that it is a combination of rights and duties: a combination designed to give the power-holder the right to perform an office, but a right qualified by fiduciary duties controlling the performance of his tasks. Only an analysis in terms of right-cum-duty can give the power a conceptual niche which is closely related to, yet at the same time evidently distinct from, an ordinary right.

Compare, to see all this better, an owner's power over his property with the power of a trustee over the property he administers. A full owner, as everybody knows, can do with his property as he likes; use or abuse it, sell it or give it away, these options all adding up to what we mean by full or absolute ownership. A trustee, on the other hand, cannot interfere with another's property unless he has a right so to do; what is more, even having this right does not give him wholly permissive options, the choice not being left to him whether to act or not. Just as a policeman not only may but in many circumstances must make an arrest, so a trustee not only may sell, he must do so if prudent management so demands. As office-holders, the trustee and policeman of course retain some discretion as to when, or how, to act in the exercise of their offices. They have this discretion because all the contingencies relating to their tasks cannot be specified in advance; yet it is a discretion which has to be controllable so as to ensure that these or other power-holders perform their tasks honestly or in good faith, and thus conform to the 'fiduciary' obligations that attach to all those managing not their own but other people's interests.

Very crucial differences then emerge as between powers and rights *sans phrase*, if only because powers combine rights and duties in the one person, whereas ordinary rights require correlative duties in another as part of a two-party relationship. Hence to describe an owner as having a 'power' to sell his property is to use that word somewhat undiscriminatingly; it in fact both duplicates what the word 'right' can say (namely, that the owner *may* sell his property), and obscures the fact that the owner has a full, not just a representative, right to sell – that is, he can sell or not sell, or sell prudently or imprudently. Conversely, to say that a trustee has a 'right' to sell property is similarly misleading since the word 'right' does not include the fiduciary or discretionary qualifications which we have suggested 'power' includes. There is another confusion as well. By including within what Bentham called 'powers of contrectation' the powers of handling a person's property, some have come to view these powers as exceptional liberties or permissions, exceptional because they are powers not everyone has.[7] But on the analysis here presented, powers are neither liberties, nor are they exceptional. Not liberties because these powers are not defensive in character, nor are they 'dutiless'; on the contrary, a trustee, appointed to administer an estate, may obtain an assertive claim for at least the expenses he has incurred, quite apart from becoming the titular owner of the trust property, thus obtaining rights against anyone interfering with it. Nor are powers exceptional in the full sense which 'exceptional' is now meant to bear. Though true that not everyone is a trustee, only some (appointed) persons are, this cannot be what is supposed to be exceptional about them. Were a trustee thus 'exceptional', would not everybody empowered to deal with another person or property also do an exceptional job? For Bentham, apparently, even an owner's right to deal with his own property was an exceptional power, though 'exceptional' may, for him, not have meant more than 'exclusive', as he also said that the law 'gives you alone a power over the land'.[8] If so, however, the question is what is not exceptional: does not every right then become a power, for is not every right exceptional and exclusive to the right-holder in precisely the same way?

It follows that if we are to make a firm distinction between rights and powers, we need to see a power not (*à la* Hohfeld) as a means of changing legal relations, nor (*à la* Bentham–Hart) as something exclusive or exceptional, but, perhaps more simply, as a right coupled with a duty or as a duty-combined right. Not only does this, and it seems this approach alone, give power a use that is non-duplicative and *sui generis*, it also reclarifies the nature of a right which can now be seen as something which, unlike a power, may or may not be exercised exactly according to the wishes of the right-holder himself. This, in a nutshell, is precisely why a person can be said to have a right but not a power to marry; for though a person may sometimes have an exceptional right or privilege to marry (if, as for example in Rome, he was a foreigner), he is still under no duty so to do.[9]

THE NATURE OF PRIVILEGE

It will be remembered that we substituted for the word 'privilege', introduced by Hohfeld, the word 'liberty', to free the former for another and, as we suggest, more correct use. What then is a privilege? Does it have a specific function distinct from that of right or liberty? The answer can be relatively brief, provided we keep to the traditional sense of privilege in which, as everyone knows, it mainly means a special or exceptional advantage, granted or belonging only to certain individuals or classes of individuals: an advantage, in short, which ordinary persons normally do not have.[10] Foreign diplomats have the privilege of acquiring duty-free goods, they also have the advantage of not being suable in foreign courts of law, an exempting or negative privilege also known as an immunity. Parliamentarians have the privilege of being able to say things which others cannot; in some countries they also enjoy an immunity from arrest. Such things as documents, or occasions, can be privileges too, but the implications of this are somewhat different. To speak of a privileged document is not to attach an advantage to it, but to classify it as confidential or secret; to speak of a privileged occasion similarly refers not to an advantage but to a proper defence or excuse for an injurious act, yet an excuse available to every relevant wrongdoer. For our purposes, therefore, privileges are best seen in relation to individuals, at any rate in any discussion about rights; moreover individuals who instead of the common run rather represent the select few. To be seated next to the

Queen, for example, is a privilege because normally regarded as a distinction of an exceptional kind; it is an advantage setting one above others. One becomes a 'chosen' individual.[11]

Where Hohfeld confined privileges to a particular niche, it is now clear that they directly parallel rights: they are in fact rights on a more restricted or select scale. A man enjoying a privilege has by definition a superior right to that held by an ordinary man just as the latter has a right superior to that of a person who is 'underprivileged'. Most rights, admittedly, are not privileges, but very many privileges are like rights. Thus those with superior legal status have rights which constitute privileges, especially if compared to the rights of those belonging to the rest of us. Also, one may have a privileged liberty-right rather than a privileged claim-right; the latter would be a right or claim to a noble title or estate, the former can be a rare permission, such as being seated next to the Queen; without such permission one would have no defence to a charge of violating royal protocol. Powers, too, can be privileged; they would then be powers only special persons can exercise. A trustee is not usually said to have a privilege instead of a power of management, but perhaps persons of high birth would alone have the privilege of administering royal estates.

Some privileges have caused greater difficulty, especially those which correspond to permissions or liberties. One has a privilege, maintains White, if one is privileged to hear Callas sing, for this enriches one's musical experience, it does not merely exempt one from a legal restraint.[12] But this example is somewhat ambivalent. The word 'privileged' no doubt lends itself to stating rare experiences of the Callas kind, but this is not what our problem now is about. To say it was a privilege to hear Callas sing is to refer to a most uncommon pleasure, but is not to state a normative fact such as having special access to a limited event. Even to say I bought a ticket for a Callas concert would give me an entitlement but again no privilege, for I would be doing what everyone does seeking admission to a concert. However, to indicate that I was an invited guest at one of her private soirées might well put the Callas-event in the same privileged category as the previous liberty of being seated next to the Queen, both these permissions being both highly special and restricted. Either occasion becomes a privilege as it enables one to experience an advantage others do not have; one here has a privileged liberty or right, inasmuch as one now has a defence to any charge of having gatecrashed a private performance or being disrespectful to the sovereign. In neither case, however, does the privilege give one more than this: I still have no affirmative claim to join the musical party or the royal entourage.

Privileges, it will then be noticed, run parallel both to powers and permissions and to ordinary rights, except that in all these cases privileges refer to the rights of persons in a special class. One can therefore call them 'special' rights, rights above the ordinary, if only to distinguish them from 'ordinary' rights with which the 'special' can be compared. Privileges, in other words, do not formally differ from rights or from permissions or powers, though they obviously do differ qualitatively as more prestigious rights. The same parallelism applies to immunities, at any rate in one of the two senses in which the word immunity is used. In this sense an immunity turns out to be nothing but the negative counterpart of the privilege; it becomes more exactly (as, for example, in the diplomats' case) a privilege-not, thus an exact parallel of the right-not. And this sense of immunity certainly performs a separate and useful role.

In a wider sense, however, immunity is frequently used to refer to fundamental legal or constitutionally guaranteed rights, those which particularly protect the individual from adverse treatment by anyone, including a government or legislature, assuming the latter do regard themselves (constitutionally) bound to respect fundamental rights.[13] Yet though true that an individual now enjoys something of an immunity against any abrogation of his basic rights, it is a mistake to think that the 'immunity' here represents something special or new; the immunity now in question is rather a right that anybody can violate, apart from such rights which only a government can break.[14] Similarly, it is a mistake to think of this immunity as being more especially related to a 'power' than to an ordinary (right–duty) right. An individual citizen is, and can only be, protected if there exist prohibitions, or duties-not, against possible interferers with his rights, prohibitions which are direct correlatives of what are otherwise known as basic (or 'inalienable') rights, which mostly are rights-not, normally rights not to be interfered with in respect of our persons, or free speech, or free assembly, or other basic freedoms from restraint. Such rights-not can of course be called immunities; however they are immunities which do not call for a special Hohfeldian square, being easily accomodated within an ordinary right–duty relationship. The specific role which Hohfeld advocated for that word therefore breaks down; the immunity ceases to be a separate concept as does also its correlative, the 'disability', and its opposite, the 'liability', the redundancy of which we earlier tried to explain.[15]

DERIVATIVE AND UNEQUAL RIGHTS

Permissions, powers and privileges yet require some further remarks. Permissions and powers, to return to them first, are rights, or cognates of rights, inasmuch as they too denote certain extensions of the word 'may'. But they are rights only in a derivative sense since, unlike primary rights, they cannot come into existence unless given or granted by someone with a right. If, more particularly, we ask how a permission or a power can at all arise, any account must stress that both permission and power emanate from one person to another, or from a grantor (*X*) to a grantee (*Y*), since without such a grant *Y* could not rightfully act in relation to *X*'s affairs. Indeed power and permission further presume that *X*, in granting either, has full rights over his own property; in fact, giving *Y* a permission or power in respect of any of his assets is merely another way in which *X* may deal with his own property as he wishes to deal with it. In giving *Y* a permission (for example, to walk on his grass), *X* will give away an advantage; in giving *Y* a power (for example, for *Y* to act as his trustee), *X* will try to extend his own managerial potentialities. In the former case *X* might be doing a kindness, though one we can still presume to be in his interest, while the grant of a power would be merely an instance of *X*'s beneficial exercise of his property-rights. What all this shows is that both permission and power are parasitic or dependent on, as they are also auxiliaries of, primary rights, or rights *sans phrase*. Two other features follow from this. One, that these various rights cannot coexist in the same right-holder, for they are quite different rights; at the very least if you have a primary right, you do not need a derivative one.[16] Two, that, contrary to what Hohfeld thought, we do not need a notion of 'power' to effect legal change. Certainly *X* must give *Y* a power if *X* wants to delegate that change; but for the rest, a person having rights can make all the relevant legal changes he wants, that is, all those changes that affect his interests: this capacity is, in fact, one of the major points about rights.

In some cases, it may be objected, a power is not derivative, as where *Y* does not obtain his powers directly but is appointed by a court to act as trustee or guardian or personal administrator for *X*. This, however, does not affect the present argument, for the court, too, cannot grant such powers unless it does so on behalf of somebody's rights; the nature of the power thus remains the same. Its derivative nature is also the same when we speak of a policeman's power of arrest or a parent's power of control or chastisement. These powers, going as they do well beyond managerial powers, to extend to one person's coercive powers over another, what Bentham called 'powers of imperation', are, according to him, retained by many persons, not only the police or parents or guardians but sometimes even 'individuals at large'.[17] What, concretely, these powers are does not concern us here. The important thing is that, on the one hand, these powers, too, are impregnated with obligations since neither policeman nor parent can exercise his rights without regard to the duties appurtenant to his public role; and that, on the other, these powers, especially those of the police, are but part and parcel of the coercive machinery of the community without which we would not have positive or law-enforced rights.

Permissions and powers as derivative rights are thus more akin to secondary *in personam* rights, and consequently quite unlike rights *in rem* which latter now re-emerge as our basic or primary rights. Permissions and powers are more like rights *in personam* because they, too, require to be specially created by contract or express appointment, or some other declaration of will, for they are rights which do not arise naturally; they only arise, it should now be clearer, as a result of our exercising basic or primary rights, those relating to property especially. In this sense, permissions or powers are even describable as essentially positive rights in that they derive, as they only can so derive, from an already recognised source of rights. Only primary rights, as we shall shortly see, may require a natural justification or foundation, precisely because they are basic moral rights.

Privileges are in a different category, for privileges, as we earlier remarked, are different from ordinary rights in being special rights. But if this is their main difference, privileges raise a difficulty of a wider sort. For special privileges are obviously 'unequal' rights in that some usually limited sections of the society thereby enjoy 'greater' rights than do other classes, a difference well attested to by well-known historical facts. In feudal times the land-owning aristocracy possessed substantially greater rights than the peasantry, so much so that these classes even turned out to be far from equal before the law; precisely the inequalities that the 'natural rights' of the eighteenth century were so militantly set against. Human beings, especially those belonging to the same political community, had begun to be seen as having, naturally, equal rights.[18] Yet the difficulty we are now after is not historical but conceptual, namely, how rights can be unequal yet still be rights. The broad answer is that rights do not always have to be equal, only particular rights have to be. Some rights can be unequal in, so to speak, quantitative or material respects. Rights *in personam* usually so differ from case to case, depending on the particular transaction between the parties concerned: *A*, for example, may have a right for \$100 against *B*; X a right for \$10 from *Y*. In a similar way, a society may allow different rights or privileges to different sections for reasons of political power or expediency, that is, there will be rights or privileges for certain persons, rights which now arise chiefly by political fiat, from above. Not so, however, natural or moral rights which, based as they are on *a priori* reasoning or rational justification, can only take shape as equal rights, especially rights as those to life and limb, or the right to hold (some) property. Our subsequent chapters have more to say about this.

7 From Positive to Natural Rights

THE POSITIVE–NATURAL DISTINCTION

Our business has hitherto been with mainly 'positive' as distinct from 'natural' rights, meaning by the former rights institutionally recognised, either legally because backed by coercive consequences, or rights recognised as part of accepted practices. These latter are often more fitful, less predictable in their remedial effects, but they nevertheless give rise to significant social censure, it being, of course, the very point of a practice that specified rights are relatively respected or observed. A positive right, furthermore, is not only an institutionally operative right, it is also a right which is contained in a 'literary' source, be this an oral tradition or a written law, sources through which positive rights thus declare their existence, the sources being those which the institutional operators recognise as authoritative.

What we commonly describe as 'natural' rights lack this institutional dimension, being neither legally enforceable nor part of a working practice or custom, nor emanating from an authoritative source. Yet if so, what is it to speak of natural rights as rights? Are they merely imperfect or inchoate rights – merely demands or petitions or pleas, what Feinberg called 'manifesto claims'?[1] Or are they, as we shall argue, rights in another, even more basic, sense of the term? Yet if so, what can this sense be? Obviously it is not enough to say that only with or under rights does each one of us obtain full stature as an individual, or that only if we do have rights do we not need to beg or plead, or even to feel grateful for what another person does.[2] Ringing statements such as these not only fail to explain how natural rights can be supported as such, they also seem unmindful of Bentham's old warning against using natural rights as a devious way of saying not that there are, but that there ideally ought to be, certain rights. What therefore has to be shown, if natural rights are to be upheld as a logically viable category deserving the name right at all, is that in stating a natural right we are not simply making a persuasive claim, but are advancing arguments that connect with deep moral principles, principles of justice we simply cannot dispense with in certain forms of communal discourse at any rate.

How moral rights thus connect with moral principles may become clearer as this discussion unfolds. To start with, however, it is important to refute a view according to which natural rights are otiose, offering (it is said) no more than a 'tactical advantage' for rhetorical purposes yet otherwise presenting no real gain over and above a direct appeal to relevant moral principles: a disadvantaged person is not really helped if told that he has moral if he has no legal rights.[3] There are two replies to this. One is that it cannot be just a matter of choosing between rights and principles, if only because 'principles' provide no adequate answer either: the disadvantaged person would not be better off if told that, though without legal rights, he is supported by moral principles. What is more, as compared with moral principles taken at large, rights-talk still has the advantage that it particularly identifies the moral principles now of relevance, these being precisely those principles which have to do with the claims of individuals *qua* individuals. Rights indeed 'individuate' the specific interests or grievances individuals are concerned with; they focus on these interests as well as give them the forensic emphasis they require relating as they do to very crucial disputes in our inter-individual relationships.

Our second reply has some unfinished business with the positive–natural distinction itself, in the form at any rate in which this distinction is usually portrayed. The important thing to notice is that positive or legal rights, for all their institutional recognition, are not quite so self-sustaining as rights as modern legal and even moral theory would have them be. If we could invariably resort to legal rights we would have no problem about natural ones, for we could then simply derive our rights from some recognised source, whether a written or oral code, it being a prime feature of positive rights that there are specified methods of ascertaining what they are. But legal rights begin to pose problems where there are textual or literary gaps in the existing sources, gaps which are not so easily filled by interpretation or construction to cover novel complaints. Because here, where the sources are totally or ambiguously silent, we do appear to need a notion of moral principles or natural rights if a judge is to be in a position to decide even 'hard' cases, not as a legislator but still as a judge.[4]

Nor is this all. Positive legal rights, with or without interpretation, beg an important question about themselves, the question, namely, why they themselves are considered to be rights. A common, but misleading, view is to see positive and natural rights as fundamentally independent of each other, positive rights being regarded as operating like specific claims for specific interests, while natural or moral rights appear more like pious incantations of little practical significance, incapable of delivering enforceable social goods. But where can such positive rights come from at all? Unless we imagine a legal system in which rights and rules are entirely imposed from above, by some omniscient sovereign, without any rational participation by those to whom rights and duties are to belong, how or why would positive rights emerge? What could be the interests or burdens they would intervene to protect? Without moral rights as their foundations, often as their forerunners as moral customs, positive or legal rights would have no occasion to appear; we would not even know what rights to attach sanctions to, let alone sanctions of the requisite severity; their enforceability would merely record an institutional fact without in the least explaining why such positive rights exist. In actual fact, it need hardly be said, positive rights, if not always at any rate more often than not, do incorporate moral rights if only because positive rights, too, include existing or emerging moral views as to interpersonal relationships. And though moral rights, having become institutionally recognised, now appear as positive rights the fact remains that the positive recognition of positive legal rights is, at least normally, itself dependent on rights having a moral content, it being this content that is taken to justify their enforceability.

For all these reasons it becomes simply inadequate to say, though this is what orthodox positivism usually does contend, that legal rights are rights because they emanate from a proper source or descend from a recognised authority. Our hard-nosed positivistic theories that reject natural rights thus miss the critically important point that since positive rights also call for an 'internal' validity in addition to their 'external' enforceability, they themselves cannot do without a theory of natural rights. If rights were in fact no more than reactions to things done, we would not need rights – it would be sufficient to speak of pain or suffering and its amends. Or, putting this in another way, if positive rights cannot arise, as it were, ready made, since they too have to build, if not in every case at least crucially or typically, on moral grounds, it follows that the difference between natural and positive rights, though admittedly not to be taken lightly, can on no account be made too rigidly. In practice, no doubt, legal rights normally appear as more proccupied with enforcement, while moral rights put major emphasis on their content; yet it would be a mistake to see in this any sort of proof that positive rights belong to a category so altogether different as to deny every deeper connection with moral rights. Hence positive and natural rights should not be seen as independent of each other, but rather as rights which somehow interrelate – which, indeed, they logically must do if there is to be any sort of conceptual or semantic link between them by virtue of which they are both describable as rights.

TOWARDS NATURAL RIGHTS

It further follows that our whole positive–natural distinction requires a fresh start, but a start which must now come from the side of natural rights. What, more particularly, has to be shown is how we can isolate or identify sufficient conditions on the basis of which natural rights can be given an independent justification and so can stand on their own feet. Of course natural rights still cannot enter the business of competing with their positive counterparts on the level of enforceability; their job is rather to provide the arguments for the moral justification of certain basic rights – the rights we absolutely need to guide us through our interpersonal grievances so as to live and let live in a community. Moreover, just as positive rights are, in their own way, necessary rights virtually by definition, given the recognised legal sources declaring them as rights, so natural rights must comparably qualify as necessary – though in their case the necessity will have to be rational as it cannot be 'literary' or hierarchical. For unless natural rights properly exist as rights, they would count as no more than rhetorical demands or pleas, at most only desirable ideals of rights. Not that natural rights have been uninfluential, even as rhetoric; they have been, as is common knowledge, a remarkably persuasive force in the history of thought, especially in the movement against absolutist government, in the eighteenth century in particular. Even this historical achievement, however, would not by itself make them rights fully or properly so called.

One or two other points need to be clarified. Although moral rights, as we have defined them, differ from positive ones in not being institutionally operative, they nevertheless do convey, as claims, that there are strong reasons for them to become operative or recognised.

Obviously to claim a right, even a moral right, is to claim something one wants to see realised. The claimant would not be claiming a right unless his claim was important to him as an individual. Nor would there be any point in even looking for a moral justification, neither any point in trying to see positive rights as emanating from a moral base, if natural or moral rights did not imply a firm claim to answerability. Indeed any such claim, precisely because it is a claim and not a mere demand or request, that is, a claim advancing itself as somehow valid or justified, addresses itself as much to the claimant's group or community as against the alleged duty-holder, simply because the person with a grievance makes his claim not only to be heard but to be responded to, this even over the head of the duty-holder if the latter does not wish to comply. This not only follows from the very nature of such claims, all this reveals, yet again, the logically close connection between claims and rights, a feature so much insisted upon already in Chapter 1. Clearly it would make little sense to state a claim requiring actions or abstentions from another if there was no possibility of having answerable claims, that is, claims which socially committed the other side either to offer a defence or excuse for his action or to acknowledge the claim as a reason for redress. There would be little point in advancing a claim for the sake of a right unless we *did* seek to make another answerable for the violation of that right: we would not understand what rights were if the claimant went about asserting claims to this, that or the other thing, without ever making an effort to obtain these things.[5] Nor would that effort get off the ground unless a community could be assumed to have an interest in aiding and abetting such claims.

This answerability makes for a crucially important social element frequently overlooked. To make claims answerable in fact requires extensive social means, because claimants, as single persons, lack on average the requisite physical means to enforce the redress they seek, nor could they ever be certain how the balance of forces might tip. The community thus appealed to may be large or small, dispersed or highly localised; it can be one's family, or tribe, or one's cultural or religious or industrial group, although for present purposes we shall, for the sake of clarity, concentrate on the normal socio-political community which, with its organisable public opinion or monopoly of force, is precisely the social body best capable of effectively responding to individual claims. Particularly such a community must listen and respond to certain grievances if it is to function as a viable entity. Its very structural viability requires a broad set of shared interests which provide both the occasion and the grounds for recognising at least some basic natural rights; without any shared interests, there would in fact be no community, and without a community no purpose whatever in arguing about rights. In this light we can almost say that certain, though only certain, natural rights, those necessary for a community to exist, become, so to speak, putative positive rights.

Thus the explanatory model now proposed is 'communal' or 'structural' in character, not a new version of a 'social contract' as might at first appear. A contractarian explanation appears anyhow a little too vulnerable to serve as a starting-point. Not because there is no good historical evidence of such social contracts, nor evidence of a constant renewal of such contracts as the contractors change with every death or birth in a demographically uninterrupted stream. The problem rather is that the 'social contract' falters even as a logical hypothesis. First, because a social contract, if it means what it says, cannot easily make room for moral disputes since, on principle, it is supposed to settle in advance everything of relevance, almost like a positive legal text. The natural rights we shall try to explain will indeed delineate a communal structure which if necessarily discursive and non-forcible in its primary purpose yet remains, or can remain, highly adversarial between individual and individual. Second, to make a contract of any kind anyhow presupposes an acceptance among the contractors of certain prior conditions, primarily those of mutual equality and freedom, without which they are in fact in no position to negotiate, or to arrive at anything even remotely resembling a free accord. This at once shows that to understand natural rights we have to understand equality and freedom as communal presuppositions, or as the broad but basic conditions without which there cannot even be true moral argument between individuals within a group. To this we shortly return, after examining, relatively briefly, other more familiar theories.

SOME DOCTRINES OF NATURAL RIGHTS

The usual and traditional approach to natural rights has been a predominantly 'doctrinal' or 'deductive' one: to think of them as having to be derived or deduced from what are taken to be 'higher' principles or super-doctrines such as 'reason', 'justice', or 'human worth' or 'dignity'. If moral rights were indeed thus deducible, the whole problem would not have been what it is; the problem is precisely how any such doctrines can function as tenable major premises. Yet as these doctrines constantly recur in connection with natural rights, we have to see why they do not and cannot work self-sufficiently; properly disentangled they may nevertheless be of some help later on.

Historically the most persistent theory has been that deriving natural rights from 'reason', from the 'dictates of right reason' in particular. As traditionally pursued, this approach is largely false, since natural rights, just like moral principles, have no special cognitive source. Reason in any case does not reveal truths about single instances, it only enables us to understand connections between instances, connections of an inferential kind; neither can we validly deduce rights from reason if this means deducing moral 'mays' or 'oughts' from premises stating matters of fact alone, which of course merely restates 'Hume's Law' – a law indeed we now can take for granted, as it generally is in modern analysis. For similar reasons, it is also a mistake to see 'nature' as a uniquely suitable source for natural rights. Though it tells us what is the case, nature does not provide standards to distinguish different values, whether prize roses, or oppressed citizens; for standards are not set by nature but human choice.[6] Thus nature does not indicate the standards we need for moral purposes; we do not morally distinguish black men from white, even if nature comprises both black and white. Often enough we even seek moral arrangements that differ from natural facts: in nature the big fish eat the small, in morals we do not expose the weak to the strong. All this, to be sure, does not in the least affect the role of reason generally. If rights are to be rationally supported we must construct an appropriate framework within which natural rights can validly operate. This, too, is an exercise in reason, now taking the form of rational analysis.

Other doctrines about natural rights advance more specific grounds in their support. A moral right, one well-known theory goes, has to meet the criteria of a *just* claim, so that natural rights call for a theory of justice, since only such a theory can justify or (in Frankena's word) 'justicise' rights; unjustified rights are at best pious proclamations, whereas justified rights do have a satisfactory moral content that justice distinguishes.[7] This idea comes essentially from Mill, according to whom we have to separate what are merely inexpedient from morally wrong acts and, among the latter, between those that do and do not violate another's right.[8] We act wrongly in not being charitable or generous when we ought to be, but we do not thereby act unjustly; to act unjustly is to breach rights towards a given individual. Unfortunately Mill does not really take us further than this; for though he maintains that to refer to a person's right is to speak of his valid or sufficient claim upon society to protect him in the possession of it, either by the force of law or by that of education or opinion, yet if we ask why society ought to defend such a claim, all we are told is that rights are supported by general utility.[9] It may well be that, on a closer reading, Mills' utilitarianism does not actually exclude individual rights, as is often believed.[10] But this still does not tell us how exactly 'utility' or 'welfare' forms a necessary basis for natural rights. For since utility is, for Mill, the eventual or residual basis of all morality, we are no longer sure what distinctive morality, even within a wider utilitarian morality, justice does represent. In fact in resorting to an ultimate utility, Mill seems to be abandoning the very possibility of a 'justicing' principle which his initial discussion somehow promised he might provide.

EQUALITY AND FREEDOM

Moral theorists have also turned to the notions of equality or freedom, both of which have certainly a great deal to do with natural rights. The idea of equality is, in one of its meanings, conceptually involved in all rights, if only because rights like rules have a necessarily *general* character, a generality enabling like cases to be treated alike. At present, however, the question is whether equality plays a more specific role: whether it can be seen as a sort of special humanistic dispensation that attributes to, or recognises in, each individual the same intrinsic worth or dignity. According to Vlastos, one very influential supporter of this view, the equality of individuals rests in the end on their individual human value, regardless of their personal merits or skills.[11] Were a visitor from Mars to ask why we want this equality, our answer would have to be that we could not otherwise treat individuals equally; for just as we love someone regardless of merit, so our moral attitude even to persons we may not love must not depend on their personal achievements. Thus the harm or pain inflicted on a nobody must be judged as seriously as injury to the highest, and a person in danger of drowning must be helped whatever his merits – contrary to the Martian, who may regard these valuations as quite absurd since, in his view, the unmeritorious do not deserve the same treatment as those far more meritorious than they.

Unfortunately Vlastos does not really explain why a moral standard of equality is strictly necessary. He is throughout arguing from *within* a cultural system which accepts equality as highly desirable, but he really does nothing to justify it. No doubt, a maxim such as 'equality before the law' cannot be made sense of unless we accord equal status to all citizens; but the question is why we should. Nor does the striking analogy with love really help. I love another because, as Montaigne would say, I am I and he or she is he or she; so I love another not only regardless of merits but often in spite of his or her faults; this has therefore little to do with equality. Neither is it really true that, morally, we disregard merit or desert, in a good number of situations at least. The unmeritorious, it is true, are not outcasts, but they are morally responsible for the injuries they do, even if we no longer, as did older societies, outlaw those we regard as too anti-social in their behaviour. Again, much of our distributive justice depends on what we deserve to have; we certainly do respect what men do with their freedom, or what they achieve by their personal striving or skill; nor do we always take men as of equal worth precisely because they are human beings with different choices and capacities.[12]

A special criticism applies to the concept of intrinsic human worth. Though meant to enunciate a humanistic standard justifying equality for all, the idea is apt to stress qualities which, so emphatically individualistic in their preferences or experiences, may support personal freedom but have again little to do with equality. If, for example, *A* and *B* listen to the same symphony, with the same delight, the word 'same' in the latter clause does not mean same as in 'same symphony' but something which in each case can be too personal to be really or fully the same. If so, the question is how these very personal emotions are to be translated into equal rights? Or, to rephrase the question, how can *A* have a right to something quite so specific as this; if nobody else can reach his standards of satisfaction, how does this tally with an equalitarian ideal or principle? So if *A*'s musical experience at the same concert is different from *B*'s, how is *A*'s right to his enjoyment to be satisfied together with *B*'s, for *B* has the same right to be so satisfied according to his own capacity for enjoyment which *ex hypothesi* is no less worthy or unique? Thus the idea of 'intrinsic worth' creates problems of 'personal' variation of absolutely no assistance to equal natural rights. The fact remains that the idea of equality can be of utterly vital help, only provided it is interpreted within more modest scope. Indeed all we need to say, or tell the visitor from Mars, is that not only have persons not the same worth, not only are persons therefore far from equal, yet there is one area in which they are, or at least have to be treated as equal, this being the area of their actions to each other, for (as we shortly explain in greater detail) unless treated as equal here they could not even argue, argue morally, about their rights or grievances. So interpreted, however, the doctrine of individual worth rather loses the particular character that theories as the above tend to bestow on it.

What is more, equality must, in the present context, not be seen as an independent moral quality, one sufficient by itself, but rather as one closely related to, even integrated with, that of individual freedom which now becomes a sort of twin-criterion. This, or something like this, was seen by Hart, although some aspects of his views cannot be left without comment. Now Hart's thesis is to the effect that there is at least one natural right, if there are any moral or natural rights at all, namely the equal right of all men to be free: a basic even if not absolute moral right that belongs to men *qua* men.[13] Speaking broadly, to be free here means mainly a right – an equal right – to forbearance on the part of all others from any action that might cause another injury or impediment. A 'general' right typically arises where we ask for the moral title of another where he interferes with us, the implication being that all men have a recognised right to equal freedom, for otherwise the justifying title would be 'wholly vacuous' since we could use any difference between people as a justification for interfering with them. To claim a 'special' right, based on a special relationship such as contract or status (parent and child), is similarly, albeit more indirectly, to invoke a principle of freedom since in advancing a contract or status right is to claim that an interference with another, unless in fact authorised or consented to, would indeed be an injurious violation of a right.[14]

Hart's overall argument nevertheless goes both too far and not far enough. Not far enough because, instead of providing a strictly 'necessary' basis for natural rights, Hart rather extrapolates from established or positive results a 'general' and 'special' right each of which is now presented as an exemplification of a natural right; the natural right itself, however, is not specially justified. And his argument goes too far in that he takes these exemplifications not as possessing a 'moral quality' but as mutual restrictions which constitute 'a certain distribution of human freedom'; it is apparently left to the right-holder's own discretion to determine whether the duty-holder shall be answerable towards him.[15] Quite apart from thus restricting rights to alienable as distinct from inalienable ones, this argument rather tends to obscure the whole moral foundation of natural rights. We are given no explanation why the 'distribution of human freedom' is or should be as it is. Suppose that distribution happened to be different (in the style, for example, of the special privileges considered at the end of Chapter 6), would these arrangements also amount to natural rights? Indeed, if freedom is to be presented as a key to natural rights, we have to see it certainly as a distinctive moral value, yet again not as a value sufficient by itself but rather as one which conjoins, as a matter of logical necessity, with that of mutual equality, an equality the two sides to a dispute must accept if they are at all to argue morally. These ideas may become clearer below.

A RATIONAL BASIS OF RIGHTS

We have said that, even though natural rights cannot be 'deduced' from reason, we still need a rational basis or framework if natural rights are to be properly justified. After what has already been said, finding a rational justification may no longer be quite so mystifying as it perhaps earlier appeared. We have to explore the particular conditions within which it not only makes sense to speak of natural rights, but in which they become an utterly indispensable device. More particularly, what we have to show is not that natural rights belong to men as men, rather that a *language* of rights is something we are ineluctably, and thus naturally, committed to, if we also accept, as for present purposes we must and anyhow do, that our social organisation, unlike that of an ant-hill or beehive, distinguishes itself by discursive features, those of mutual argument and moral answerability. The essential point is that a language of rights excludes, categorically so, any imposition of burdens upon individuals by the exercise of physical force or by mental pressures amounting to duress, excepting of course the application of force for sanctionable or remedial purposes, the latter obviously measures which may arise at a later stage, as an additional form of pressure on the part of the community; but they are not measures which determine whether there are to be rights in the first place.

The crucial consequence of this is that our moral discourse about rights, presupposing as this does a nucleus of interpersonal forbearances, must then avoid giving reasons for our actions which convey any sort of superiority by one over the other, whether a superiority of physical power or that of other means. Which in turn implies that, as they argue, both sides to the argument must in giving reasons to each other also accept, or for the purposes of the argument at least admit, that the two arguers are equal at any rate as arguers. For unless they assume such mutual equality, the reasons they will give will not be proper reasons, they will merely tell each other what to do, even if their so-called reasons somehow conceal the fact that they are not arguing but pressuring each other verbally. The equality now referred to is thus but another way of protecting either side against interference or compulsion, so also a way of safeguarding each side's physical or personal immunity. It is, in other words, a predominantly negative rather than a positive equality mainly serving a person's freedom, a freedom the practical foundation of which is precisely the equality of the weak with the strong.[16]

Negative as this equality is, the reasons now given in argument must correspondingly observe a number of requirements if the reasons are to be relevantly arguable. A principal requirement therefore is that the reasons have to relate to actions, to what one does, not to what one is or has. One cannot give a reason for being white or black, strong or weak; one can only give reasons for what one does or does not do. A risqué story, for example, can make a maiden blush; but hearing the story is rather the cause for blushing, not its reason, for she cannot blush at will.[17] The action must, so to speak, be mine to allow giving a reason; consequently, giving reasons for action, unlike giving reasons for appraisal, involves a notion of what it is to succeed or fail since we are trying to explain why our action produced this result instead of that, the assumption being that an action is always personally avoidable.[18] Likewise, the reasons we give cannot be simply statements about one's own aims or preferences, but must relate to actions which affect the burdens and benefits between two individuals, actions which affect the *status quo* obtaining between them. If *A* sees *B* wasting his own money or time, *A* would have no reason to intervene, however irritated or outraged he may feel by what *B* does; for if *A* could intervene he would be able to manipulate *B* according to his own wishes or views of life which might not be shared by *B*. You cannot guide another in the same way as you educate a child or train a dog; such conduct would make *B* an inferior, denying his equality.

We then see a notion of mutual equality, or equality-cum-freedom, embedded in the very discourse of rights. Not that we have to suppose that human beings are all alike; it suffices to admit that they are negatively alike, alike as objects of non-interference, or as subjects of negative freedom, whatever their other personal qualities. It also becomes clearer why moral discourse has now to take this two-fold form: why, on the one hand, we have to eschew non-action or purely appraisal reasons, for these become strictly irrelevant if only because one cannot argue about, in order to change or avoid, a person's qualities or attributes – only our actions can change, which is indeed why we do argue about them; and why, on the other hand, two sides cannot even begin to argue about their actions unless they assume a discursive equality between themselves. To see this better, imagine two persons negotiating with each other, whether these negotiations result in an agreement or not. So long as they are negotiating, arguing, reasoning together, they must respect each other's position equally. Even if one side happens to be stronger than the other a genuine negotiation presupposes that the stronger cannot impose his will on the other, capable as he may be of doing that. So just as in the market-place we can imagine a course of dickering, one party saying the object is too costly, the other that it is too cheap, so here, in our moral situation, there are certain counters which each side may use, the one to complain, the other to defend, if they are to qualify as relevant or rational arguers. Of course we must not drive this analogy too hard: negotiation may include persuasion, cajoling, even taking advantage of the other's error, whereas an argument about rights takes a very different course, concerned as it is with a new grievance or detriment brought about by another's conduct we suppose to have been avoidable. Of course if the detriment occurs unavoidably or inevitably, there could in fact be no grievance or complaint as there would be no responsible agent whose actions might be properly criticised.

There is more. With a status of equality now assumed between the parties, this not only justifies a claim by one against the other, it also makes the other answerable to the former. This answerability, either by admitting responsibility for a claim or by advancing defences or excuses for an action, now becomes a pivotal element. If, as between *A* and *B*, *B* were to refuse to make an answer to *A*, he (*B*) would thereby not only reject *A*'s grievance but would in effect deny even *A*'s equality with *B*. For in refusing to answer *A*, *B* would change the nature of their relationship; instead of allowing *A*'s grievance to become the occasion for an argumentative exchange, *B*'s present denial to respond would, albeit implicitly but no less effectively, declare *B*'s superiority to which *A* would have no option but to submit unless he were to react forcibly, in which case however the contest would no longer be resolved by argument but by the stronger of the two. If, however, we assume that *B* fully plays the discursive game, as he often does and as our communal or institutional arrangements anyhow constrain him to do, we witness the emergence of those basic natural rights we have been speaking about. For *A*'s natural right against *B* now lies precisely in *A*'s claim in respect of harm done to him by *B*'s action, as well as a claim coupled with *B*'s answerability on the basis of their mutual freedom and equality.

NATURAL RIGHTS AND MORAL ARGUMENT

It might be objected that the above explanations bear obvious marks of circularity in that they seem to be justifying natural rights in terms of a particular (a severely negative) equality, while, conversely, they appear to justify equality not for its own sake but only as a necessary foundation for natural rights. There is undeniably this element of circularity, but it is not a vicious one. Like many another explanation of an analytic kind, any such process of explaining keeps us moving round and round, as we seek to construct a rational framework within which a concept like natural right can validly operate – a framework, moreover, that requires us to link up ideas which, as they are not self-evidently related, can only be connected if they turn out to be mutually supportive. The ideas have to support each other like the stones in an arch.

Again it may be objected that the above explanation begs an important question, since it stipulates an end or aim which is assumed rather than justified. All we have shown, this objection might continue, is a form of reasoning which shows why we have to do *x* if we are to achieve our given end *y*, which only shows why *x*-ing is necessary to produce *y*, but not how or why *y* is necessary in itself. Though we need to know about *y* in order to be able to reason about *x*, that is, how *x* can achieve *y*, as in all such reasoning of a general kind, this still says nothing about *y*, which remains a given datum beyond reasoning, thus little more than a mere value preference.[19]

This latter objection, if it bases itself on Hume's Law, however uses this law much too extremely, in the present context at any rate. For our business at present is not with purely personal values or preferences or passions which admittedly reason cannot demonstrate. Our business rather is with common social data, our main question being how, or under what conditions, we can engage in a form of argument which we usually call moral argument, that is, argument we must engage in to settle our inter-individual grievances discursively, living as we do in peaceable human communities. The alternative to this would be to arouse forcible or compulsive attitudes in some, and submissive or supine reactions in others, none of which however furnishes any basis for the sort of interpersonal parity which alone makes moral rights-talk possible, let alone appropriate. To state a claim or right would be pointless if the other person at whom a claim is directed could simply disregard the complaint just by refusing even to listen answerably.

What we said of the relation between two persons, applies, *mutatis mutandis*, to a community at large, the former bilateral relationship being merely a sort of cellular paradigm of the wider social grouping. So a community must persevere with the same non-forcible or discursive conditions of resolving grievances, indeed must do so in a regular or systematic way. It must do so because, unlike a dispute between a particular *A* and *B* which may be isolated or infrequent, or anyhow insignificant, in a group interpersonal grievances tend to be continuous, since because of the greater numbers there is not just one but many pairs of *A*s and *B*s. Unless a community performed this task, protecting its members' rights to live, to go unharmed, to keep property, or to make complaints, there would be little or no purpose for rights: social organisation would be a form of life in which the strong control the weak, without very much occasion for talk about morality.

To stress this communal background is by no means to submerge the individual, or to say the community or society comes first, or that the needs of the individual must be determined by the needs of society. On the contrary, the whole point of relating the individual to a community via a notion of rights is to make society into a sort of guarantor of relatively peaceable conditions under which a person can live in relative freedom simply because he can argue as an equal amongst other individuals. Suppose we adopted (perhaps persuaded by our previous visitor from Mars) a decidedly meritarian policy in which only the élite, but not the so-called riff-raff, would have rights. The former would now be able to dispose of all those who, because of lesser achievements, fail to measure up, and, for that very reason, are declared to be rightless. So the élite, respecting only merit, however assessed, could hunt their inferiors as farmers hunt rabbits or other undesirable pests. Nor is there, on principle, any limit to this process of selection. The merits may change as fashions do: today the *A*s may hunt or enslave the *B*s; tomorrow a section of *A*s may do the same against other *A*s suddenly declared inferior. Such total meritarianism then transpires to be a policy which, carried to its ultimate conclusion, becomes a prescription for self-destruction rather than for maintaining any sort of community. Such communities as survived would be based on preferential contingencies, and not on moral principle which is not liable to change in the same way, its aim being precisely to preserve a community by maintaining the equality of its members, through maintaining the rights of the non-preferred.

If the above analysis is even broadly correct, it may throw a little light on the notion of justice, or at least on some aspects of it. Mill, it will be remembered, thought the *idée mère* of justice as that of conformity to law, the law comprising those rights and duties which are positively established and enforceable.[20] There is no inconsistency between these positive rights and the view of natural rights propounded here. For Mill could have said, even if in point of fact he did not, that his legal rights reflect justice not because their positivism gives them a new ('just') quality, but because they are, so to speak, the positive successors to those moral rights which, as we have tried to show, keep the balance, a discursive or argumentative balance, between the strong and the weak in an ongoing community. In this light, justice can then be seen not so much as indicating a special state of affairs or a particular source of morality, a source yielding specific insights or intuitions as to what is just or unjust. Justice might here more simply be viewed as a discursive method, as broadly descriptive of the moral arguments we employ and must employ to manage our adversarial disputes, mainly those relating to life, limb and property. And these arguments will be steeped in natural rights precisely because they cannot avoid appealing to the notions of equality and freedom, the very notions which, we have tried to show, have to be presupposed if an argument about individual rights is to be carried on. Seen in this way, it seems easier to explain also why it is that whenever we discuss 'justice' or try to define it, we immediately break it up into other notions, in particular those of equality and freedom. The reason is that these notions are amenable to argument in ways that justice, taken as a single idea, is not. Equality and freedom thus seem to lie at the heart of justice just as they lie at the centre of natural rights, if only because in the one case, as in the other, they are the notions that determine our moral discourse about other-regarding actions giving rise to answerable grievances.

8 Life, Limb and Property

INALIENABLE AND ALIENABLE RIGHTS

We will have seen that natural rights, far from merely an historical inheritance, are indispensable logical tools if moral grievances are to be argued rationally, given the social organisation we have or want. These natural rights consist above all of those protections or immunities which secure the individual's free and equal position amongst other individuals, with their central emphasis therefore on the rights to life, limb and property, all of these most necessary conditions if a person is to be able to pursue his life compatibly with the similar interests of others. The rights to life and limb refer to a person's physical or mental integrity: he is to be free from compulsion or other avoidable interference, whereas the right to property extends this immunity to things, or assets, sometimes opportunities.

The question immediately arises whether these basic rights equivalent to immunities are basic even to the extent of being 'inalienable', thus becoming rights we cannot renounce, unlike so-called 'alienable' rights which the right-holder may waive or modify. Now there certainly are rights which are alienable just as a right-holder deems fit. So you can waive or renounce a debt just as you can make a gift of your money or anything else that is yours. Similarly you may choose not to initiate a private legal action (for example, in tort) since such actions are best left to a person's discretion, the assumption being that certain types of harm affect people differently: what to one may seem harmful, another may treat as less intolerable. At first sight, it may even appear that 'alienable' rights are more fully, or more genuinely, rights than are 'inalienable' ones, if only because the former possess permissive dimensions which turn rights into 'normative property'.[1]

It is important to see, however, that alienable rights are essentially derivative in nature. Their alienability always reaches back to, as it depends on, the prior existence of basic rights. If tort-actions are renounceable, this is in point of fact limited to relatively minor wrongs, where as regards major torts which coincide with criminal felonies proceedings can be taken out of the hands of the right-holder, since criminal proceedings take precedence over private suits.[2] And if transactional or *in personam* rights are waivable, this, too, derives from a more basic right, that to property, for the right to waive would not be intelligible unless we had property or assets to dispose of. The actual practical worth of transactional rights lies precisely in their being alienable so that they can function as assets to be traded or transferred. But this does not change their theoretically derivative character; only if his basic rights are secure can a person freely exchange his things or services with others. So if we put aside such alienable rights as minor wrongs or such which are contractual or transactional rights, we see that basic rights are generally inalienable; such rights would in fact mean very little if they could be easily given away; alienability would defeat their very purpose as protective rights. It is then a mistake to see rights as essentially 'normative property' rather than as basic protections for individuals. It may well be that alienable rights are the more important, statistically or practically; but practical appearances must not be allowed to distort theoretical reality. For the purposes of an analysis of rights it is the inalienable, not the alienable, right that should be seen as the primary paradigm.[3]

Some may still object, specially those for whom rights are normative property, that to see inalienable rights as our primary rights, in particular the inalienable rights found in the criminal law, is to overlook the important feature that a right permits one to do or not to do a thing as one pleases: only alienable rights, on this view, possess this optional amplitude precisely because they are modifiable or waivable at will. But this objection makes a confusion between two somewhat different rights, between what we may call an asset-right on the one hand, and a protective right on the other; or between a right operating as a transactional tool, enabling you to confer assets or advantages, and a right which identifies the basic interests protecting an individual, especially interests without which an individual would be permanently diminished. Precisely this protective role makes basic rights inalienable; we would simply not effectively protect someone as an equal and free individual in a group if his equality and freedom were merely optional.

It is, moreover, this protective feature of (inalienable) rights which explains the limitations upon our freedom to make self-restrictive or self-harming choices, even though we often think the right to make such choices is what personal freedom is about. So there are limitations upon our consenting to personal injury: we cannot give up our right not to be killed or maimed, or sold or subjected to slavery. Killing or maiming another, even with his consent as in a duel, or assaulting another in an act of sexual sadism, have been held to be criminal wrongs.[4] The harm done in such cases is far too unbeneficial to be consented to. In many situations, it is true, one can definitely agree to harm, or what would otherwise be an injury; here the consent negatives the ground of complaint since you cannot both consent to some injury and complain of it; the maxim of *volenti non fit injuria* covers precisely this.

Even so, and this is perhaps not sufficiently realised, the consent must bear some relation to the harm done, in the sense that the consent must normally be only a means of gaining some personal benefit or advantage, it cannot operate as *carte blanche* for the commission of grave personal injury. This indeed ties up with an earlier point: that a person cannot claim to do something as of right if the alleged right is, conventionally considered, of no possible benefit to him: a murderer has accordingly no right against his executioner to be hanged. Thus even strict libertarians like Mill do not see freedom as a licence not to be free. While they do not object to such self-restrictive consents as contracts or marriage, they will not accept a person subjecting himself to slavery; for this would constitute too extreme a change in status since the would-be slave could expose himself to circumstances utterly beyond anything envisaged in his original consent.[5] Nor of course does a person, by voluntarily committing a serious crime, thereby waive his right to life or liberty; such a person is not waiving a right in the sense of exercising it; what he does is more simply to incur a punishment.

The upshot is that basic rights, those to life and limb and, to some extent, also the right to property, cannot be alienable if basic rights are to have enduring effect. They are simply the rights an individual must have if he is to continue as both a free and equal individual in his community. Thus when Rousseau declares that the true objection to slavery is not that it makes men unhappy, for some men are not unhappy as slaves, that the objection rather is that it is unworthy of human beings to create such forms of life, what he had in mind was perhaps not equality for equality's sake, but maintaining the individual in a community of equals; only in a communal context does it fully make sense to require basic rights of life and limb so as to ensure the equal freedom of each individual.[6]

Can it be said that 'inalienable' is here the wrong word anyhow:

that it would be more correct to speak of 'indefeasible' rights, since only these can, if at all, be overridden on moral grounds, while inalienable rights only deny that they can be abandoned or altered by their holder.[7] Still this differentiation is more terminological than real. The reasons which prevent a right from being alienated are virtually the same as those which strengthen its indefeasibility, nor is there any good reason why inalienable rights should not be similarly overridable. Of course to override inalienable (or indefeasible) rights would require particularly strong moral grounds, for anything less would diminish their nature as basic rights. In practice, the only grounds capable of overriding such rights are grounds furnished by competing or conflicting rights, a matter to which we shortly return. For the moment the overall point to stress is that to speak as we now do of natural or moral rights is to refer to inalienable rights of this basic sort. Alienable rights, by contrast, are not only derivative, depending (as we earlier said) on prior basic rights, they are typically positive and legal: nobody would wish to acquire a right to a debt against another, for example, if that right were not legally enforceable as such.

PUBLIC NATURAL RIGHTS

The basic rights we have identified as applying as between individuals apply with no less force to the relationship between an individual and his government. Just as the rights to life, limb and property represent, so to speak, the very bastion of an individual's position *vis-à-vis* another individual, so the same rights operate against public officials. In fact, basic or inalienable rights are today advanced not so much in respect of persons intending to sell themselves into slavery as, rather, against governments attempting to restrict the free activities of citizens. Just as private basic rights imply that an individual (*A*) cannot be interfered with by another (*B*) without *A*'s consent to *B*, provided such consent does not itself undermine the very purpose of the basic right, so a government, or the persons exercising the powers of government, cannot intervene in *A*'s life or projects in an arbitrary manner, that is, without *A*'s valid consent, either express or at least impliable. It is true that in this respect private and public natural rights work out a little differently since the respective interventions may relate to different spheres of an individual's activity, but their logical basis is very similar. Also, the idea of personal consent as expressed in the maxim *volenti non fit injuria* is, when everything is said, not so far removed from the idea of no taxation without representation.

Nor is it at all necessary to isolate or identify a separate right to liberty as obtaining particularly in the political realm; for every right implies as a right a relevant measure of freedom, if only because a right indicates, at least in this sphere, a sort of protected immunity, that of being entitled to be left alone as an individual. On this basis it is by no means the case that all citizens have or must have as their so-called democratic birthright a sort of natural right to liberty applying to all people anywhere. What would be truer to say is that citizens have basic immunities against interference, that is, rights which protect their choices to speak, or to be silent, or to assemble, and so on. Like private natural rights, such public rights, too, are best stated negatively, for the simple reason that their main purpose is protective, to protect a person's normal integrity, including that of his home and his normal activities. In English law, in fact, fundamental constitutional rights were mostly established by aggrieved citizens bringing ordinary actions in trespass against offending government officials, the latter sued in their private capacity.[8]

Some public rights are a little more difficult. At first impression it seems obvious enough that every citizen should have the right to participate fully in the affairs of his community. Though some political opportunities are, in the nature of things, restricted (not everyone can be King or President, not everyone even a member of parliament), everyone's right to vote has long seemed essential. A person, says an old legal case, cannot be prevented from voting, for common citizens 'have a great and considerable right in the government, and a share in the legislative without whom no law passes'.[9] Here the right to vote was upheld under an old constitutional practice, to deny which would have been to treat that citizen as an inferior. Yet admitting all this, even admitting that disfranchised citizens might be exposed to greater oppression than those freely voting, this still does not mean – and this is the major point we are now really concerned with – that voting is a natural right, as natural as the rights to life, limb or property earlier mentioned.

Consider, to pursue this a little further, a society in which the right to vote is limited. Suppose a voting system under which illiterates have no vote, the full vote being confined to the educated. Such a system often is symptomatic of other inequalities, such as inequality before the law, but this need not always be so. Just as we sometimes opt for quantitative restrictions (for example, two-third majorities), so we may prefer qualitative restrictions which may exclude illiterates for purposes of government. What is more, the latter may accept their disfranchisement with profound indifference; they may agree that they are as little qualified for political office as for the priesthood, a situation indeed observable in older hierarchical societies. This by no means entails that those without votes cannot be free and equal in all other respects so as to enjoy all other moral and legal rights.[10] Those both voting and elected may even regard themselves as representatives of the whole community, including those disfranchised. In this way, restricted voting is not necessarily an indication of political or moral oppression just as abstaining from voting is not always irresponsible.

The fact remains that the possibilities above outlined may be quite exceptional, wholly dependent on the voluntary acceptance by all of a measure of inequality. As soon, moreover, as this particular consensus changes, demands for full equality may insist on full political participation by all sections of the community. What all this shows is then simply this: that 'equality' can operate on different levels, depending on the equality sought. On a most basic level we certainly cannot dispense with an absolute if negative equality of life and limb for a human community to exist, irrespective of the wishes of its members as to how free or equal they care to be. But on a purely political level equality allows of not inconsiderable ('alienable') variations. A right to vote, for example, can be variously restricted; it is therefore not necessarily a basic right, but is only contingently one, entirely depending on the social views or consensus in a particular society.

BASIC RIGHTS AND THEIR MORAL DIRECTION

Arguing as we have been that natural rights toll for the individual, indicative as they are of a basic moral structure of our inter-individual relationships, these rights do not however possess definitive normative scope. Not because their underlying principle against external interference is uncertain, but rather because the nature of that interference may itself be in question, either because another's action may prove to be less avoidable than appears or because the alleged harm may, in a real world, seem more trivial than significant. Still so long as the action is deliberate and the damage manifest, there can be little difficulty. A victim of a deliberate robbery may obviously complain of the assault on his person and property, just as there are countless other instances of intentional harm a 'free' individual must be protected against: morality could not even begin without such freedom or immunity being recognised.

Difficulties however appear as soon as we go beyond this type of harm, to extend our rights to life and limb to cover harmful interferences caused by less intended actions or by consequences actually unforeseen but not perhaps unforseeable. Here we enter a more 'open' area, one where we are no longer quite so certain how far, or how insistently, we can object to external interferences. We enter a realm of moral ideas not with static but dynamic boundaries. And here our natural rights also subtly change; for these rights are no longer quite so 'natural' in the sense of being 'necessary', that is, necessary in a strict sense, as furnishing the only foundations for basic equality and freedom amongst individuals. In this more 'open' area, it will be seen, our 'natural' rights rather depend on further moral choices a community may care to make. What can such further choices be? The answer is that our basic and necessary natural rights, having laid the moral foundations of life in a social community, also indicate – indicate, not dictate – the broad direction along which any new choices must be made. For, prismatic as they are with moral innuendo, natural rights provide an overall moral bias towards the individual's protection, and thereby towards his personal wellbeing, a bias obviously flowing from their insistence upon an individual's freedom, his freedom from harm especially. Like ratchet-wheels, natural rights allow new choices to move only in one direction: now not back, only forward.

Natural rights, moreover, given their moral direction, can fill up 'open' areas through extensions by way of new rights which connect with, as they rise upon, the basic rights. Indeed, unless these extensions can be so nourished from a source of basic rights, the new rights would operate in a moral vacuum, for it is our basic natural rights which provide the discursive vehicle for any reasoning about new rights. Without their basic moral bias, including the moral direction they offer, it would not even be possible to have moral reasoning in relation to the new rights, for such reasoning cannot operate without standards in terms of which our new rights can be supported or justified. Our justificatory reasons, more particularly, have to show that the new rights we allow on the basis of the old are not simply 'invented' or 'decreed', but that they morally connect with what has gone before: that new rights are thus 'in line' with previous rights. Our basic natural rights, given their moral bias, then not only give us reasons for possible further rights, in so doing they also encourage new lines of moral thought: we can go forward with greater confidence.

As we so go forward, furthermore, the new rights we allow bear this peculiarity: that though, in their moment of inception, they are natural rights, if only their own justification relies on reasons and not on 'sources', at the moment of their 'declaration', so to speak, they become positive rights. They turn into positive as well as legal rights, for one thing, because inspired though they are by the moral bias of our basic natural rights, the new rights are, as already said, not strictly necessary rights but contingent on the actual degree of freedom or wellbeing a community would wish for its members. The new rights become positive, for another thing, because being contingent rather than necessary, they have to specify or certify themselves as rights, since of course, once declared, they are rights applying to everybody in the same (universalisable) position, not just to the one person succeeding in his lawsuit. On this analysis, therefore, what we have called strictly natural rights, that is, both necessary and basic moral rights, only furnish the moral framework, the essential 'theme' of justice, without which we could not even have a community of free and equal individuals: without which, consequently, we would not even have a social context within which rights-talk could at all take place. Positive rights, on the other hand, though they rest, directly or indirectly, on basic natural rights, can in turn be seen as 'variations' of the latter; they are thus relativistic rather than necessary rights if only because a community may always change its legal relationships, always provided it does not disturb its own basic framework of a community of individuals. While, in other words, a social group must have rights to life, limb and property if its members are to have rights at all, which is why we call these (necessary) natural rights, it is different with regard to other rights, such as rights to privacy (for example, a right to a room of one's own) which both depend on current social choices and require to be positively specified if only to indicate the extent or scope of the choices we make.

CONFLICT AMONG BASIC RIGHTS

There are situations in which basic natural rights may mutually conflict. Now conflict does not mean that in exercising his freedom, or pursuing his own interest, *A* happens to invade *B*'s interests which conduct results in injury to *B*. For *A*, we assume, is always free to act in his own interests; the question is precisely whether he also has the right to interfere with the right of *B*. Hence to say that *A* has a right to be free, generally only means that *A* is to be free from interference, not that he is free to interfere; to have such freedom to interfere he must have a special defensive right, or at least some power or privilege, which however are not the rights now relevant. Thus to constitute a conflict *A*'s right must, in its exercise, conflict with *B*'s right, each right being supposedly equal, the question only being which of the two rights is to have precedence.

The problem of conflicting rights is sometimes confused with the notion of *prima facie* rights we encountered earlier.[11] *Prima facie* rights are of course meant not to be absolute but qualifiable or overridable in appropriate circumstances, except that *prima facie* rights do not themselves inform us whether, and why, they are in fact overridable, even where two rights conflict. To know this, we first need to have some idea as to which might be the stronger right of the two; yet to adjudge upon their comparative strength we also need some standards to refer to. However what can such standards be? The following examples offer some assistance.

Suppose a situation of extraordinary famine, or other circumstances of public emergency. Such circumstances often make normal individual rights quite unfulfillable as well as distinctly less significant.[12] So, in a community hit by famine and threatened by death, its members still do not cease to have rights, including rights of property. But any one member will lose his right to inordinate amounts of food he may have laboriously hoarded or dearly bought, the emergency being such that he has to share his food with others. Not that such an individual can be deprived of all his food since he too must survive; for as his own food is now distributed to enable others to live, so these others – or the community as a whole – must respect his own right to life. Or suppose a situation in which some citizens have to be quarantined for a contagious disease; though their basic rights to liberty are now overridden, this again does not mean that their rights completely disappear. Their rights retain a residual strength; in fact, they now operate, admittedly somewhat indirectly, to give those affected a right to be treated at least as considerately as circumstances permit.[13] Or take a person seriously injured in an accident; his emergency now overrides other people's normal right to clear traffic; to attend to an injured man is obviously more important than to enable others to get home. Or consider a person who is solemnly promised an urgent loan by his friend, only to be told that the latter cannot oblige because of a sudden and costly illness in his own family, an illness which must take precedence over other engagements. Or consider, finally, a case (we mentioned in a previous chapter) of someone having to return a gun to its owner, but then refusing to do this as he becomes aware that the owner is a madman intending to kill an innocent person.

The above situations tell a most interesting moral story, throwing a good deal of light upon the ranking, more implicit than explicit, of our moral priorities. In the accident and gun cases a person's right to life or health takes precedence over the commuter's liberty to get home in time, or the friend's expectation of the money or the borrower's duty to return the borrowed gun. In these cases it is the right to life or limb that is accorded a higher order than other rights competing with it.[14] A commuter, for example, cannot protest at his inconvenience on the ground, which might be true, that the injured man is dying anyhow; the latter still retains a right that everything possible be done for him. Of course a right to life cannot always be given a total priority. There may be obvious physical or medical unfeasibilities, or there can be other circumstances such as a disaster threatening a whole community in which case scarce medical resources are reserved for more probable survivors. Such extreme cases apart, however, an individual's right to life or limb, including urgent medical attention, is usually regarded as coming first among virtually all other entitlements. As our examples show, life and limb come before liberty as well as before property. Unless we rated life and limb more highly than liberty, we could not justify preventive detention or other measures for the sake of public health; and unless we put the former above property, we could never open, even in times of famine, the private granaries for the benefit of all citizens. Unless, more generally, we adopted such ranking, with right to life and limb at the top of our moral list, it would even be difficult to make so simple point as that a major injury deserved more urgent treatment than a minor one.

Sometimes, it will be obvious, our moral ranking may be too problematic to allow clear preferences. This is particularly so where our rights compete not between 'higher' and 'lower' but between rights of the same order. And here the conflict cannot be resolved by reference to a moral scale. If the conflict is between 'life' and 'life' we are caught by a dilemma of tragic proportions for which we have no real solution. If the conflict is between 'lesser' rights, between 'property' and 'property' or between equal material interests, we shall have to decide according to the view we take of the relative harm in each set of circumstances, sometimes appealing to such ideas as 'public interest', sometimes to utilitarian or 'consequentialist' considerations, to help us tip the balance. Here, however, we would be dealing with much wider moral choices, indeed choices which have to do with the survival or the best interests of a collectivity as a whole. They are social choices which therefore fall quite outside the ambit of individual rights.

THE RIGHT OF PROPERTY I

As a person has a natural right to life and limb, so he has a right to exercise control over external things with the same right of non-interference. It is only through this latter right that we can appropriate or possess things, that things can become mine or thine. At first sight it looks as though a great deal more is involved in a proprietary right. Unlike a right to life and limb which we earlier described as purely negative, a right of property looks more positive as it is a way of acquiring the goods of life – which immediately raises the question of how a thing can indeed 'become' one's property, or how on rational grounds we can assert that something 'belongs' to one. Now it is true that a right of property carries acquistive overtones; also true that words like 'acquiring', 'belonging', 'owning', and so on, are convenient expressions where our concern is with the location of a title or the commerce of goods. But, so we shall argue, the basic question about property is not this, but one more straightforwardly negative, namely, at what point a person does obtain a right of non-interference against others in respect of goods over which he claims control. In the case of life and limb this point of non-interference arises, so to speak, naturally for all individuals endowed with a normal sensibility or sensitivity to pain. In the case of things, however, the point of non-interference has to be established somewhat artificially, by way of a special rule to create a special nexus between a man and a thing.

Two aspects of the problem should be kept apart. First, there are things which you may be in the process of using or consuming, or which you wear or carry. To deprive you of the bite you eat or the clothes you wear is as much harm to a person as it is an offence against property; to deal with this aspect we would not need a separate right of property. Yet we do require a distinct proprietary right for our second problem, namely, where we claim a *res* not for purposes of its immediate consumption, but as part of our intention to exercise over it more remote or constructive control: as where we wish to retain a tract of land not for prompt use or cultivation, but nevertheless with every intention of keeping it. Or (to put the problem by way of what looks like a different case, yet is one which raises essentially the same question) suppose that *A* and *B*, both assumed to have exactly the same needs and merits, dispute the possession of a certain object: how can such a possessory dispute between them be decided rationally? Not, it will be clear, that we have too many alternatives of determining this, especially if we assume that there is morally nothing to choose between the disputants themselves. Of course one easy solution is to toss a coin, but this would be too aleatory an approach, not at all the moral or juristic answer we look for.

Another alternative is rationally more satisfactory. This bids us to adopt a technical rule of the kind long familiar in European jurisprudence, at least since the time of Grotius – a rule to the effect that something belongs to the first or 'original' rather than to any later occupier of a thing. Hume, who was much occupied with this matter, thought it 'just' to annex title to the first possessor since 'first possession always engages the attention of most'.[15] This alleged 'justice' of the rule may at first sight seem a little spurious, if only because we are now assuming complete moral equality between A and B. Nor, to be sure, does the present rule derive from any such justification as, for example, a Lockian labour-theory which of course gives the property to a possessor who mixes his labour with a thing. Hume, though by no means opposed to a labour-theory, correctly saw it to be inapplicable to present purposes, if only because any possessor, not only the first, could be a labour-expending one.[16] But as Hume also saw, the first-occupant rule is anyhow adequately explained by saying that there is no colour of reason to assign the property to any succeeding occupant. For unless we attribute possession to the first occupant, whether it be land or a seat in a theatre, a second person could dispossess the first, a third the second, and so on indefinitely. The rule, in other words, is what Hume might have called an 'artificial' one, artificial or technical in the sense that it enables us to settle this sort of dispute without the occupant merely saying 'what I have I hold', which would be tantamount to a taking without advancing any justification at all.

The above is, needless to say, not our only rule of acquisition; there are various others, such as rules prescription, accession and succession. But these latter are, strictly speaking, only secondary or auxiliary rules as they anyhow depend on there being a first occupant from whom an accessive or successive title is descendable. An heir, for example, acquires title because he is, so to speak, conferred it by the bounty of the first possessor. Similarly a person taking or acquiring a *res* under prescription or accession takes the place of a first occupant, occupying as he does with the explicit, more usually the implicit consent of the current owner, which obviously again assumes there is someone with a prior right, otherwise no title or property could be ceded or transferred so as to hold good against any possible claims of others. It is true that, as a matter of social fact, disputes about first occupancy are nowadays very rare since acquisition now commonly takes place by purchase or by gift rather than by original possession. The fact remains that, logically, we could not (apart from such methods as drawing lots) have a right to property without a rule giving the first occupant the right of continuous possession. We must, in the final analysis, begin with such a right if we are to have a right to property in the first place.

THE RIGHT OF PROPERTY II

So far we have been analysing the right of property as such, seen in its negative dimension, how it is that even external things may give one a right to non-interference by others. To give such a right is, of course, to say nothing as yet about its quantum, about how much property a person may have. Since, moreover, our basic right to property rather confirms a person's freedom of acquisition, and since property comes unequally to individuals if only because of the different ways in which they exercise their freedom, the right of property may give rise to significant inequalities. Having a property-right is not to be in any way obliged to seek equality with the next man: property-wise one need not keep up with the Joneses. In this sense, a person only has the quantity or quality of property he goes out to get and so wants or deserves. Accordingly, we have to distinguish between two rights of property, between an *equal right* to property on the one hand, and a right to *equal property* on the other.[17] The latter right gives everyone the same, or substantially the same, making us all more or less alike. Not so the former which, in stating that everyone has the same right, merely states the obvious: that unless there is equality in this sense, that is, the sense of no-one having a greater right than another, there cannot be any moral rights or rules. An equal right of property, more particularly, implies that the poor man's right of property is exactly the same as the rich man's, for though he may happen to be poor, or choose to have less than the rich, his right to acquire must nevertheless be the same, as regards both quality and quantity; for if not, their respective freedoms would no longer be equal.

If a person need not, as already said, keep up with the Joneses, even if he must remain free to do so, it nevertheless seems a mistake to suggest that 'logically' there is nothing objectionable in saying that everyone possesses the property appropriate to his race or colour.[18] What does seem logically wrong with this is that the 'equal right' given to everyone is flawed in this crucial respect: that it presupposes an equal opportunity of acquiring property which now turns out to be intrinsically unequal. A person is denied his freedom to acquire goods for reasons which have nothing to do with his capacities or interests or actions and everything to do with essentially unalterable qualities. Accordingly, it may not be quite enough to say that if two people have rights to unequal amounts of property, there must be 'some difference' to justify it: not enough unless we are very clear that the difference in question itself corresponds to a moral principle; that, as we have seen in Chapter 7, the reasons given for the difference are reasons of action, not of attribute or appraisal; for to give any of the latter reasons would be to falsify the very logic of equality as it is supposed to apply to the situations we are considering.

The equal right of property, together with the right of equality of opportunity underlying it, then tie up with the natural right of freedom as we have tried to explain it. An equal right of property gives each individual a freedom to act without interference just as it allows him to fend for himself. Consequently we can even say that individual freedom would not be quite freedom if everybody were inevitably and invariably given the same. For the freedom (or liberty) now being considered, apart from its negative protection against interference or spoliation by others, is also a sort of positive freedom, positive in a self-realising or fulfilling or creative sense. What a person is, what property he has will depend on him, on his own effort to the extent that he wishes to exert himself. Indeed, to say that a person is free means that it is left to him to what extent he wishes to exercise his options which, at least on principle, are the same for everybody. Thus acquisitive freedom now presumes each person's ability to work out his own economic salvation, the right of property being completely neutral about the quantity or quality of the property a person acquires. All this, it almost goes without saying, tells only part of the total story. As we know, free societies often give rise to profound and prolonged inequalities, not just as regards conspicuous consumption but even in the distribution of bare necessities. The question therefore is whether the principle of an equal right of property allows of further argument to allow some measure of relief, at least for those who happen to be poor. The next chapter discusses this.

9 Rights to Welfare and Other Benefits

WELFARE RIGHTS: FIRST STEPS

Whereas the natural rights we so far discussed were of a 'negative' or forbearance-oriented character, the rights we shall now consider have to do with 'positive' benefits of a material or financial kind. The right to welfare is a pre-eminent instance of this – a right, incidentally, now often described as a human right, although the actual difference between this and a natural right is usually left rather nebulous, unless it be that human rights are presumed to go beyond the traditional rights of man, to include various social or economic rights, such as a right to leisure or to holidays with pay, in fact rights now declared to appertain, more or less like positive rights, to all citizens, at any rate those within the United Nations.[1] As in these pages we try to delimit a tighter or strictly rational conception of natural rights, we shall continue to speak of a right to welfare as a natural one, preoccupied as we are with the question of how, or how far, such a right can itself be justified as tenable.

Any human being, it is worth repeating, has to make his own life according to his capacities and his wants. We are not all equal, nor do we want to end up with the same lives. What distinguishes our humanity is that we can and do accept personal differences and that we can grapple with them through moral argument. Yet even if it is false equality to make us all the same, there are differences that are humanly damaging and deeply affect our inter-individual relationships. A person, for example, can, through no fault of his own, suffer misfortune: illness, accident, or economic loss, can seriously disable his possibilities of acting or working. In some societies such personal disasters are absorbed by the extended family, but in others including ours, governed not by 'kin-law' but 'rule-law' (to use the apt Anglo-Saxon words), obligations of support do not extend beyond the nuclear family. A wife or child may claim maintenance from the husband or father; yet no other individual has a like claim against another. Hence a person commits no breach of duty if he selfishly refuses to share his gains; he certainly commits no obvious injustice if, for example, he retains the total crop of his orchard without sharing so much as an apple with his closest neighbour, even if the latter's garden has yielded nothing. Such is our sense of pity that at first sight we are tempted to think it morally impossible to deny a person a right to help if his needs are manifest. We may even accept a duty to be charitable as well as accept blame if we fail to live up to it. But this is not what our question is about: what it is about is whether a neighbour or any other person in need can claim appropriate assistance as a matter of right alone.

To investigate this further, suppose a poor person (*A*) asks another (*B*) to support him (say) with various necessaries. Here *B* can say that *A* has no right against him, for the fact that *A* is poor cannot impose any moral duty on *B*. Nobody denies that *B* might well assist *A*, make him a modest or even generous gift for which *A* might feel grateful; what is denied is that *A*'s claim for support constitutes a right. Even if we admitted that *A* was more deserving than *B*, the latter could still retort that this can be true with regard to many others, all of whom might turn out to be less deserving than *A* and, perchance, even less deserving than *B*. More generally, *B* may say that *A*'s misfortune, not being due to his (*B*'s) action or fault, is for that reason alone of no direct concern to him; that he (*B*) already has himself and his family to keep; so that to act as a stranger's keeper, however deserving the stranger, would undermine his own right to regulate his life according to his own autonomous wishes.

The moral position between *A* and *B* is further brought out by the example of the miser discussed by Hume.[2] Imagine *B* is a miser, rich, foolish and childless, and *A* is poor yet utterly deserving, the father of a numerous family; also suppose that *A* disputes *B*'s right to some article which *A* needs more than *B* does. At first impression we have little doubt to whom we would wish to give the property. To return it to the miser would gravely disappoint the poor man, as well as be against the public interest, *B* being far less likely to use his wealth productively since *A* would at the very least be supporting a numerous family. Even so, Hume contended, the property must go back to the miser; it is even 'just' to return it to him simply because it is his property, it being better to maintain 'inflexible' rules of property as this is more advisable in the long run. For adhering to firm and lasting measures, even if this is to accept the good with the ill, is more useful than to succumb to momentary but constantly 'variable' solutions. Hume indeed concedes this approach not to be entirely just, yet nevertheless advocates it as institutionally or utilitarianly the more preferable. However this contrast between the utilitarian and the just is not very convincing here. The dispute between *A* and *B*, arising as it does in respect of an article which already belongs to *B* as proprietor, is by no means so clear-cut a cleavage between justice on *A*'s side and utility on *B*'s. Undeserving as *B* might in many respects be, he is 'deserving' enough to qualify as owner, having satisfied the basic rules for the acquisition of property. Given these rules, *A* cannot 'justly' claim to be more 'entitled' to the article than *B*; for even if *A* is more deserving generally, he is not more deserving under the rules of property, precisely the rules Hume himself had equated with justice.[3]

There is yet a wider argument against allowing *A* a claim against *B* only because he happens to be the poorer, namely, the argument that this would make nonsense of the basic rules governing property. Suppose *A* is regarded as poor and *B* as rich merely because *B* has a coat which *A* lacks. If *A*, as the more deserving, now gets *B*'s coat, the rich–poor relationship is immediately reversed since *B*, left without a coat, becomes instantly the more deserving, so also entitled to (re)claim the coat. And this game can be played indefinitely, there being no logical end to it; our rights relating to property here become so quickly changeable as to be illusory. Though *B* might have a loaf of bread, he would not have it with a right to keep since *A* could always snatch the bread as soon as he happened to be hungrier and so more in need and deserving than *B*. It follows that notions such as desert or need, though they furnish (as we shall shortly see) appropriate criteria for *re*-distributing property, do not offer workable criteria for establishing an original right of property, precisely because, unlike the acquisitive rules (as that of first occupancy discussed in Chapter 8), notions such as desert or need do not assign a permanent or exclusive, but at best only a highly terminable, right of user. The fact is that distributive criteria cannot really work unless they do include firm rights of property; they cannot just work to produce effects which (as in the *A–B* example above) are mutually or reversibly expropriating. A right to welfare, as we are about to see, certainly involves changes in the properties held by the 'haves' and 'have-nots' respectively, but these changes require quite a different – in fact a public – approach.

RIGHTS AGAINST COMMUNITY

The preceding discussion will have shown that one individual (*A*) cannot advance a private right of welfare against another (*B*), however great *A*'s material needs or however urgent. Still, though *A* cannot have a private claim, he might have a public right, a right against the community. Against the latter the serious objections we identified in relation to private claims do not exist, but this alone does not show how a public claim for welfare can be justified. It is often the case that a community is far better positioned to respond to *A*'s claims than any one individual, assuming that the community is able and willing to raise sufficient common resources out of which *A*'s pressing needs can be met. Only a community acting as a body politic can mobilise enough resources since it alone can alter or override private property-rights, say by opening private granaries in times of famine, or by imposing special taxes or levies to deal with social emergencies such as natural disasters or unemployment. The point remains that this ability to organise resources cannot by itself create rights against the community; we still have to explain why an individual, even poor, ought to have a public right to welfare, and that he ought to have it not just for pragmatic or expedient reasons (for example, that it is 'better' to do something about poverty either to prevent possible disturbances or to increase the state's economic or military power), but on solid moral grounds.

Of course a community or its members may all be so charitable, or self-sacrificing, as joyously to share with others all the possessions others may need. For such highly moral people, however, we hardly require moral principles; these we only need where, in our everyday world, people are consistently more selfish and self-regarding. It will also be clear that to justify a principle or a right for the poor we have to proceed as before, namely, by unlocking the presuppositions of a natural right and, in particular, its presuppositions of individual freedom and equality. In this light consider again what the poor man's complaint consists of. His grievance is that his poverty puts him in a position of serious inequality in relation to other persons of the same group. Without this egalitarian element it would indeed be difficult to identify the moral ingredient in *A*'s complaint, for only if *A* can make a claim to at least some equality with others does his grievance become answerable at all. It has been maintained however that, in connection with poverty or similar social ills, what we invoke is not a 'strict' principle of equality but a more 'rhetorical' one: rhetorical used non-pejoratively to indicate that the wrong to be righted is poverty, not inequality, for the equality we do achieve in alleviating poverty comes as a by-product rather than as a direct goal.[4]

This can be a little misleading. Admittedly, if I am hungry I seek to still my hunger, not to be equal with those whose hunger is already stilled. Nor do I complain of hunger or poverty if, like Robinson Crusoe, I have nobody to complain to, however angry I may be with my fate. However, if as a poor man I make a claim for some assistance, my making of that claim implies a contention that my own social state should be less unequal compared with that of others than it is. The poor man is not just issuing a moral grievance that his poverty diminishes him as a man (he may do that too); his claim is rather that he is entitled to at least some of the surpluses available in the community – or, more precisely, available through the community from those of its members who qualify as 'haves', it being these who have relatively more than their actual needs compared with the 'have-nots'. We are, in other words, faced with conditions usually described as those of relative scarcity where relevant resources are neither absolutely scarce nor over-abundant but where there are nevertheless sufficient surpluses to satisfy everyone's most pressing requirements.

As these surpluses are, so far, only the property of the haves, the latter may raise strong objections to their now being called upon to make sacrifices for others. The poor man, they might object first of all, can claim nothing as of right if only because each individual has to be left to his own destiny, unfortunate as this may be. For to require one class of individuals to support another would diminish the former's freedom, they now being compelled to render an amount of 'forced labour' for other people.[5] What such views overlook, nevertheless, is that freedom does not belong to an individual in the same way as his eyes and ears belong to him; freedom rather is a right that appertains to a community-belonging individual since, as we tried to explain in Chapter 7, it is only as an equal member of a community that he can argùe to be let alone by other members of the same community. The poor man's complaint, in fact, addresses his own community; he now purports to speak as an equal to equals, not to a collection of strangers; the poor man's claim thus comes from within the community which alone enables rights to exist at all – or, more precisely, to be advanced as arguments – including the rights which attribute freedom or 'separateness' to an individual. Outside a community an individual would be no more or no less free than his own physical capacities would guarantee him; only within a community, as an equal individual amongst other such individuals, can he make a claim, whether to freedom or to (some) assistance.

It also follows that at the very least the other members of the group cannot refuse to listen to the poor man's claim, or to shrug off his grievances. To refuse to answer, or to decline having a moral dialogue with him, is to behave arbitrarily, to treat the other as an inferior, virtually to disqualify him as an equal member of the same community. What is more, if we thus disqualify the poor, if they are not to be full members of the community, at any rate not members with whom rights-talk is engaged, we cannot expect them to honour, except in the breach, the rights of others, those of the haves especially. Since, so the poor may further say, moral rights rest on their arguability, any such rights collapse if argument ceases; and if rights collapse all that remains for them to do is to seek such relief as they need through self-help, using such force as they can muster, or get away with. Historically, it is true, the poor have not normally had a right to support even if they may have been assisted as a matter of charity or generosity. This also means that, morally as well as politically, they scarcely possessed full communal membership. They shared their lives with the haves, territorially and in other contacts, but they were otherwise outsiders.

Even if the haves do agree that the poor man's claim is answerable, their answer might still be determinedly negative. For they might say that, far from treating the poor arbitrarily or unequally, the fact they are poor is not the result of what they (the haves) have done; they only succeeded in making themselves better off, without the least intention of reducing anyone to poverty. Further they can say that in doing what they did, they were not doing more than exercising their equality of opportunity which the poor, too, were never denied. This equality indeed assumes that everyone does not necessarily have the same; for were we to give to each an equal share, we would not even have to ask whether we have each the same opportunity; equality of opportunity would become literally redundant, were it our purpose merely to distribute everything equally. A 'just' community, the haves may conclude, certainly must ensure equality of opportunity, but it has no duty to do more.

Such arguments, too, the poor man should be able to counter, to the extent he needs to at any rate. In particular he must reject the insinuation that he could or should have tried harder to be less poor, and so reject any suggestion of some fault on his part. To blame him for his poverty, he will say, is to confuse extrinsic with intrinsic merit:

there can be no real blame because what happens is due to the mechanisms of a market economy. Demand conditions can change unpredictably, hence markets will not always ensure due rewards for actual effort just as changing demand may suddenly throw people out of work. Similarly a sick or incapacitated person may say that while his sickness deprives him of the sort of opportunity he might otherwise have, to deny him even a modicum of support is to treat him as if he were ordained to go under, when the community, with possibly little effort, could still offer means of subsistence and survival and therewith also another chance.

More importantly still, the poor man can say that the haves present a version of equality of opportunity which is far too narrow because too negative. Their version in effect does little more than duplicate rights we already have, that is, rights against interference, with the result that it does not give sufficient weight to the idea of opportunity itself. An opportunity, surely, is an occasion which, among other things is to help us to procure a positive benefit; it is not just freedom from interference which merely removes preliminary obstacles. Every right, so this argument may continue, even if generally negative in its import, must still carry with it some opportunity with more positive emphasis. Because a right is not (as we saw in Chapter 1) self-executive but is performative-dependent, it thus requires not only to be claimed but also the forensic possibilities of being claimed. This is why equality before the law is such a crucial condition of equal rights; and this, too, is why we feel dissatisfaction when told that courts of law are as open to everybody as is the Ritz Hotel; for this produces a situation where only the rich can afford legal redress. In this light even negative rights require more positive or equalising opportunities, if they are to function as proper rights; without supportive opportunities such rights simply become empty or illusory, as they become rights without effective duties since the duty-bearers would now have little to fear if the right-holders are sufficiently poor.

Once, moreover, we allow equality of opportunity a more positive or supportive role as opposed to a purely negative one, we remove an important impediment to the poor man's claim for a chance to survive. Nor is such a claim altogether new in moral thought. On the contrary, arguments in favour of a wider notion of equality of opportunity, together with arguments in favour of subsistence and survival, have been sustained in various contexts, though contexts on the face of them so unrelated that their convergent implications have not been fully perceived. Locke, for one, would not attribute rights of property to any man, though he had mixed his labour with it, unless 'there is enough, and as good left in common for others'.[6] Locke was obviously concerned that everyone should have their economic chance, not just the fortunate few, with the others condemned to unproductive poverty. For a similar reason we spontaneously opt for opening all the granaries in conditions of absolute scarcity. So if in a famine there are only 100 loaves of bread for 100 starving men, the only solution we (or rather the starving men) can at all defend is that each man gets one loaf; only this ensures that each man survives. Some of these ideas also appear, albeit less directly, in the doctrine of inalienable natural rights we discussed in Chapter 8. As we there saw, inalienable rights deny a person's option to abandon his rights so as to diminish or degrade himself to a state of irrevocable inferiority. The real point of this surely is that inalienable rights, though usually only concerned with the physical security of the individual, yet stem from a wider purpose, namely, to maintain a functioning community of equal individuals. Thus inalienable rights imply the recognition of a basic equality of all members of the group – not, to repeat, an equality that insists that all men are the same, but an equality that recognises that some members of the community should not be so grossly inferior in their material condition as to vacate this equality for all practical purposes.

THE QUANTUM OF WELFARE

Even if we grant a natural right to welfare for the poor man, the problem still is how much welfare he may claim. Essentially there are only two approaches of which one, that of absolute or strict equality, would, we have repeatedly observed, lead to inappropriate results. Treating everyone the same would be the right course with regard to common or collective things, be it legally joint property or a conventionally common thing such as a birthday cake. Here, as lawyers say, 'equity is equality', so that in dividing up such common property each claimant would have a right to an equal share. But this is not the case here. To give everyone the same in this context would in effect be like treating them unequally: individuals would be regimented into a mechanical uniformity that pays scant attention to their different contributions or their different needs and wants. Thus, for the Greeks, inequality was not unjust *per se*. Because if, as Plato said, equality is given to unequals the result is inequality; inequality is only then unjust, as Aristotle implied, if the measure by which we judge a person's due is comparatively disproportionate, and so in fact more arbitrary than that of an equal standard applying to all.[7]

The haves, furthermore, may remind us that what they have was not only acquired according to the accepted rules of the game, but that they deserve to retain relatively more than those who acquired less if only because what is to be distributed is largely the fruit of their enterprise, without which there would be no surpluses from which the have-nots are to profit. The reminder implies also a warning that a system of absolute equality may turn out worse for the have-nots. For getting less, the haves may have less incentive to produce, so that sooner or later there would be fewer distributable surpluses. Thus the poor man, if he is wise and not merely angry or envious, would not suggest that since he is poor everybody should be poor equally. Since he is, in any case, seeking more for himself, he would have no wish to destroy the goose that lays the golden eggs.[8] This, at all events, seems the simplest explanation of why absolute equality has generally been seen as too utopian to be actively pressed.

We are therefore left with the second alternative, that of relative equality, which also poses the difficulty of determining what the appropriate quantum of welfare should be. In fact, relative equality is bound to meander between the opposing interests of the haves and have-nots. The former, arguing as producers in terms of their own optimum freedom, seek to keep as much of their wealth as possible; the poor, on the other hand, argue in terms of their equality, their equality with others, if only to improve on their evidently inferior chances in life. Thus unlike our basic natural rights – those of life, limb and property – where we saw the ideas of equality and freedom working in tandem because there they worked negatively, in relation to the present right to welfare – with its clearly positive dimension – equality and freedom rather diverge. They diverge, very simply, because on a distributive level, equality and freedom translate into more antithetical criteria, namely the (equality-oriented) need of the poor as against the (freedom-oriented) merit of the haves. Which, of course, immediately raises the question of how we can reconcile the claims of the welfare-needy with the claims of the surplus-makers.

On a very general level this reconciliation is not difficult to make; given the moral considerations we have noticed, it comes down to assisting the poor with the essentials or necessities of life. These, it will be obvious, refer to the needs of a person as distinct from his wants, for his needs depend on 'objective' or observable phenomena and so comprise highly specific things the claimant cannot provide for himself, things like food, shelter, medicines, and so on, quite unlike personal wants or desires which include things far more 'subjective' in kind. A need for subsistence is usually so obvious that there can be little dispute as to whether a person is, or is not, requiring it. Even so, it may still be difficult to quantify these needs, to determine the exact cash value of what an individual should have. Here we will often appeal to a notional standard, that of the 'normal' or 'average' man, to discover what our normal necessities are. The poor man, needless to say, can still remain wretched since the assistance thus extended will remain modest, not to say minimal, excluding all luxuries such as drink and so on.[9]

The trouble is that what some consider luxuries, others may regard as necessities, just as some may say the community should provide more welfare, others that the community can afford only less. 'Welfare' thus turns out to be an 'essentially contested concept',[10] a concept we may argue about inconclusively, even without arguing past each other or disputing each other's evidence, simply by never agreeing about our moral appraisal of the given facts. One side may of course succeed in converting the other to their own views, or views may change with new conditions. If, for example, privacy is today considered an obvious and important need, not a mere luxury, this was by no means so in earlier, more robust, times. Again, today we accept that to satisfy human needs includes having regard to human potentialities, especially those of children whose development will suffer if special assistance is withheld.[11] Education is a necessity for the modern child who can no longer make its way in the world unless it can read and write, and has other passable skills, provided by a considerable period of education, quite unlike the aborigine child who picks up his arts of survival (for example, his skill at tracking) growing up in the tribe. But providing (public) education still leaves the question of how far we should go to enable a child to compete on reasonably equal terms, having regard to its social disadvantages, family or racial background and so on. A community cannot help children in the selection of their parents, nor endow them with the ability they lack. Perhaps genetic engineering may one day make this possible; how this would affect individual freedom is not a matter we now have to discuss.

In spite of these practical uncertainties our initial and broader point, our point of principle, still holds, namely, that a poor man's right to welfare can only be justified as a natural right if limited to essential needs. We may disagree as to the precise assistance to be given in many a case, but the notion of basic needs or necessities at least concentrates opposing ideas into a more manageable discussion, where otherwise they might flounder towards ethical extremities. However this may be, the view now adumbrated, confined as it is to basic necessities, decidedly stops short of seeking a 'fair' distribution of available goods and services. Fair distribution, as everyone knows, has been a main concern of Rawls. According to him we must, starting from an 'original position' or from behind 'a veil of ignorance', always give preference to equality, save for inequalities which are morally permissible if, but only if, they work out to everyone's advantage, or at least without detrimentally affecting the least advantaged amongst us.[12] The approach we have pursued, by contrast, did not presume the goods of life to be already available, almost like the books in a public library, so that all we need is a plan of fair shares for all. The present approach has been more concerned with what is morally involved in dealing with surpluses, which not only represent the efforts of free producers but also the only common stock out of which the needs of the poor who make no productive contribution, or not enough of it, can at all be satisfied.

There is of course no categorical objection to giving the poor more than their necessities. But this would have to be a political decision: a community, acting through its legislature, may introduce very generous welfarist or meliorist measures, including measures of affirmative action or of reverse of benign discrimination in favour of the disadvantaged. In its human generosity or desire for human wellbeing, any such measure would certainly qualify as highly moral, even if tinged with prudential considerations aimed at minimising worsening frictions between groups otherwise too alienated or hostile. Still, political decisions are contingent on majorities whose views can change as these majorities change. What we have tried to show is that there are solid arguments justifying a natural right to welfare, a right arising in favour of the poor irrespective of political decisions which may or may not be taken.

RIGHTS TO OTHER BENEFITS

We will have seen that a case for a natural right to welfare is so strictly limited as to exclude, automatically so, any right to other benefits or advantages. The needs we have spoken of are needs confined to the necessities or essentials of life, that is, necessities like food, shelter, health and so on. The mere existence of a need, does not in any case create a right to its satisfaction, although we often suppose the opposite, being here misled by an ambiguity. To say 'I need a good car' is different from saying that 'I have a need for a good car'. To need, as a verb, merely describes my wanting something for a purpose; to have a need, need taken as a noun, refers to an essential need – what one must have as a human being.[13] Similarly, you may need (want) luxuries for a purpose, but you would not be said to have a human need for them as a matter of basic welfare. In short, 'to have a need' implies 'to need', but 'to need' does not imply 'to have a need'.

Certainly the well-known maxim 'everyone according to his needs' is a tempting ideal, but it is not a very practical one so long as we live in conditions of relative scarcity, in which the commodities we have a need of are not, like air, abundant but depend on the material effort or financial sacrifices that others make. Which is but another way of saying that only certain needs can be argued for as giving grounds to rights, by no means all needs. It follows that the notion of needs cannot have the importance that moralists often imagine it has. Take, for example, the somewhat special case of praise. Everyone, it is sometimes said, has a right to a just distribution of admiration or approval, given not to oneself but to one's work or performance. Can one then have a right to praise in the same way as one can have a right to subsistence? The brief answer is no. There can be no such right on the basis of needs, at least not 'need' as we have defined it here. To give praise means to 'measure out' to people what economists sometimes call 'psychic income'.[14] This is income, however, which comes as an addition to pleasure, not in satisfaction of an urgent human necessity. It would at all events be absurd to claim praise as of right, thereby to insist on getting it, when its giving is not so much a matter of duty as one of grace and generosity. Now it may well be that a person may have a 'right' to praise of a more utilitarian sort. Our society does honour selected persons; nor is there any doubt that praise can have beneficial results as it may greatly encourage creative effort especially for achievements for which society has no other reward. To select a person for praise we of course have to ask how his deeds of work compare with the achievement of another, a question that cannot be answered unless we have a utilitarian consensus as well as something of comparative scale. But this would not be a question that asks what is due to an individual *qua* individual; it is more a question as to whether a person has, or has not, won a prize – a prize in the social competition for public recognition or acclaim.

10 The Limits of Rights

CHILDREN'S RIGHTS

We have, almost exclusively, been preoccupied with the rights of the normal adult person, as it is mainly for and around him that we look for a coherent theory of rights. The question is whether rights obtain also in relation to more peripheral subjects, such as children, lunatics and even animals. It is an important question as it raises afresh several basic issues having to do with the limits of rights. Since, as we have seen, to have rights involves a capacity to make claims or pursue interests, how can we attribute rights to those without normal capacities, including the very young or mentally handicapped who lack the intellectual capacity even to appreciate rights? Still it has long been accepted, both in law and morals, that a child has rights just as has the lunatic. What we have to discuss is why, theoretically, this should be so.

The child is often said to occupy a special position, because it is the kind of human being it is, very different from a mere vegetable or animal: 'its coming into existence involves a possessor of rights coming into being'.[1] This seems too self-fulfilling a definition, for it is still not clear how we overcome the particular difficulty of the child's lack of capacity. Were we to adopt the so-called will-theory of rights, which puts great emphasis on a person's capacity to claim and exercise his rights, the child cannot but be disqualified as a right-holder, however human it is. Now the will-theory does not deny that children have to be nurtured and cared for, that they cannot be harmed, or that they have to be protected by their parents or guardians; yet it is difficult to see how that theory (or, for that matter, the choice-theory according to which rights are a sort of normative property) can, given its tenets, allow children's rights even if it does recognise their needs or interests. Nevertheless the general legal position is that children do have rights and that what parents exercise on their behalf are inherently children's rights, so much so in fact that children cannot waive any of their basic rights so as to 'let off' their parents. Similarly, the legal or administrative measures which take away or modify parental rights are not instances of waiver, but rather ways of penalising a parent for his neglect or violation of his child's rights.

The central difficulty therefore remains, namely, how we can say that, in view of their actual incapacities, children do have rights, indeed have inalienable rights at least to nurture and care? This difficulty, admittedly, is seldom raised, so much are children's rights taken for granted virtually everywhere. If at all questioned, the usual reply is that as children they have interests, and having such interests they therefore also have rights. But for many reasons, many of which already adverted to before, this explanation will not do. It will not do even in the more sophisticated version of the interest-theory which MacCormick has more recently advanced.[2] For him, children do have rights simply because they have needs, interests and desires which can only be satisfied by parental care. We may of course disagree as to the extent of a child's legitimate needs; but these are, here as elsewhere, inevitable disagreements which in any case do not affect the general reason which supports or justifies the attribution of rights. Thus, as MacCormick is also concerned to show, a child's rights arise prior to the parents' duties; for it is not simply that every child ought to be cared for so as to bring up better or more contented person, it is rather that they have a right to care because of their needs as human beings. Just as a child may have a right (say a right to a legacy) before the corresponding duties have vested (the testamentary executor may not yet be named), so it is because children have a right to care and nurture that parents have the duty to care for them, breach of which duty would therefore constitute a wrong. Indeed, it makes more sense to put parental duties in this way than to say that children have rights because parents have duties.[3] On this basis, then, children have rights because they have interests, interests in the form of basic needs and wants which their parents (or guardians) must satisfy and which, if not met, result in great harm to the children's health or even survival.

Yet MacCormick thinks this answer not entirely adequate; he does not wish to tie the notion of 'having rights' too specifically to (what he calls) the 'want-regarding' categories of needs and interests; in fact, he regards this connection with wants as the characteristic failing of the interest-theory. 'It is uncontroversial that satisfaction of needs, interests and desires is a part of "the good" for individuals, but it is controversial whether it is exhaustive or constitutive of the good.'[4] But these hesitations appear a little strange. In the first place, even a small child can hardly ask for more than to have his needs met and his infantile interests satisfied. In the second place, it is not true that interests are entirely want-regarding; what is true is that very young children may not actually *have* interests, but, as we saw in an earlier chapter (Chapter 3), something can *be* in one's interest even if it is not wanted. It is, in fact, only on this basis that we can at all attribute interests to a newborn child as yet quite incapable of having conscious desires or wants. However, MacCormick proceeds to offer a new formula especially designed to be more 'neutral' on the moral question as to what constitutes the good, the new formula being that 'to ascribe to all members of a class *C* a right to treatment *T* is to presuppose that *T* is, in all normal circumstances, a good for every member of *C*, and that *T* is a good of such importance that it would be wrong to deny it to or withhold it from any members of *C*'.[5] Unfortunately this formula only creates further problems. On the one hand, it suggests one can have a right to any number of 'goods' in addition to needs and interests, provided they are of great importance to a class-member. On the other, the formula, far from rectifying the interest-theory, vastly extends it: anything or anyone (presumably animals or things also) can belong to class *C* and thereby acquire a right to treatment *T*. The new test seems simple: the more important the good, the greater the right attributed. Not only can our present questions not be answered with a formula of such breath-taking generality, but no such formula is indeed required, this for the simple reason that the 'good' in question cannot 'in all normal circumstances' be other than the interests or needs of children, that is, the interests in care, health, survival we already identified.

Now we here defend the interest-theory not, to be sure, to suggest that, properly presented, it might support the existence of children's rights; the intention rather is to show that the theory, however presented, cannot by itself support the creation of any rights, whether in relation to children or any other individual. As an earlier chapter tried to explain, interests only indicate, in very general terms, the sorts of benefits one individual can claim from another, whether as his due or by way of his protection; interests, however, do not automatically give rise to rights, for only certain interests do and, especially, only such interests which have a particular moral quality, a quality such as is possessed by our basic natural rights, such as the rights to life, limb and property.

As we have also tried to show, our rights-talk presupposes rights as operative only in the context of claims made by individuals upon other individuals in a discursive community. Indeed it is just this communal dimension which now plays a special part in relation to children as well. The brief explanation is that children have their typical rights not because they 'have' them, as individuals have them through their claims and arguments, but rather because children have rights *conferred* on them, to safeguard them as potential members of a community. Unless a community does replace its members, so to speak, continuously, there would be nothing else it could do to maintain its existence over time. In fact there would be little point in having rights since rights would now be confined to a discrete set of persons, constantly diminishing both numerically and temporally, with the result that a community would never be a continuing but at most a purely passing phenomenon, like a meteor.

Hence it must be a permanent part of our human endeavour to replenish the human community, the best source of new membership obviously its own children. Without capacity at first, children come into existence with the capacity to become normal adults; their incapacity thus is only temporary, their transformation as inevitable as the effluxion of time. Furthermore, only because new members regularly replace those departing is it possible to speak of a normal adult person as a type; in terms of flesh and blood he too is but a transient figure that begins with childhood and ends in death. In this light, children obviously do not constitute as separate a category as are plants or things or even animals in relation to the human group; they are, on the contrary, most closely, almost 'organically', involved with it. To give children rights is then only another aspect of how a community maintains its continuity, now by the recruitment of potential individuals of (in due course) normal capacity. This potentiality also explains why certain protective rights are extended to the unborn child, the child *en ventre sa mère*, as it is described in law; it, too, will in due course not only come into existence but become an increasingly rights-talking member. The foetus, needless to add, remains exposed to the mother's rights over her own body, including her right to an abortion as she herself thinks fit. Whether or not she has, or should have, such a right is a different story beyond this enterprise.

CONCERNING OTHER RIGHTHOLDERS

What we have said of young children applies, very broadly, to incapacitated adults. So long as there is a chance, even remote, of a medical cure or improvement for any human person, his position as right-holder cannot be altered, his right to life and limb especially; for so long as there is a chance he remains a potentially full member of the community. The situation is obviously different where a person is so mentally or physically disabled as to leave, medically speaking, absolutely no hope for him. In this case, it does seem to be pointless to attribute rights to what is in effect a human vegetable. 'Without awareness, expectation, belief, desire, aim, and purpose, a being can have no interests; without interests, he cannot be benefited; without the capacity to be a beneficiary, he can have no rights.'[6]

Yet there may be other reasons why even such a person should not be too easily disposed of, even painlessly. Not only is our right to life far too basic to be tampered with, we do not, it would seem, completely trust the dividing line between who or what is, or is not, incurable so long as we have faith in medical progress itself. Hence to argue for a right to life, even for a life we admit to be without dignity or purpose, is in effect to advance something of a prophylactic principle. For in now maintaining this right, we are protecting not so much the interests of the incapacitated as, rather, our own sensibilities as well as fears; and we are also cutting short a discussion we do not know to resolve in any case. Indeed our doubts again reveal a communal perspective; again we insist on a right to life lest we in any way endanger it and therewith possibly the very foundations of the community we live in.

It is similarly a communal viewpoint that can persuade us, if anything can, to attribute a particular significance to physical things, whether things of great artistic merit or things forming part of our environment. To resolve to preserve such things is of course to wish to restrict our ordinary tendencies towards destruction or neglect; to preserve works of art, or historical monuments, or our natural heritage, is to transpose our aesthetic values on to a cosmic scale, a scale embracing not only our present but also future generations. We may feel we are under some duty to those following us, to leave them a world worth living in as well as one that continues at least some links with earlier human or natural history. Important as these sentiments are, they still have no business to be treated as rights. Not only are we now attributing rights to entirely inanimate right-holders, we are creating at best 'vicarious' rights, rights which merely express the wishes of those who control the protected things. To speak of rights is now misplaced also in another respect. We cannot say what in one or two centuries, perhaps more, human interests might turn out to be, neither therefore say what sacrifices are immediately indicated lest present generations incur the wrath of future ones.

THE ALLEGED RIGHTS OF ANIMALS

Whether animals have rights has been much discussed in recent years. A traditional view holds that to attribute rights to animals would require the admission that the mouse has rights against the cat, the cat against the dog, and so on, all obviously absurd results.[7] More recent moves, however, have tried to bring animals within the 'interest principle', the idea being again that if it can be shown that animals have interests, one could then give them rights also, since to allow them interests would put them in the same category as children who have interests and therefore rights, rights claimable on their behalf by their representatives. This view calls for a little further examination as it re-agitates some basic conceptual issues in relation to rights.

To show that at any rate the higher animals satisfy the 'interest principle', mainly two arguments have been put forward, one by Feinberg, the other by Singer, both of which we shall come to reject. For the former, interests must be compounded of 'conations', a way of saying that subjects with interests must possess faculties of volition and desire.[8] This test quickly excludes mere things such as stones and other lifeless objects; it also excludes plants, trees and so on, for though true that the latter are not lifeless, they have no conative life, no active or conscious desires. Plants, and so on, still have needs: a tree needs water for without it it will die, yet even if we refuse that need, we would not, as far as we know, be cruel to the tree by causing it pain or suffering; refusing trees water would merely prevent them from growing, or from completing their organic cycle, but they have no sensibilities to be hurt. However animals (cats, dogs, horses, to name only those we immediately think of) do have, in Feinberg's thesis, a conative life in that they have desires and needs: they do not want to be hurt and they do want food when hungry. Singer's thesis is not dissimilar as his argument is also to the effect that animals have interests because they can suffer; feeling pain is thus a sufficient condition for possessing interests.[9] Animate subjects are in this respect utterly different from inanimate. A stone does not have interests because it cannot suffer; incapable of suffering, there is nothing to take into account; hence the question, as Bentham put it, is not: can animals reason? or can they talk? but, can they suffer?[10]

Against this it has been argued, notably by Frey, that such animal capacities or desires or needs are not sufficient to constitute interests. His main objection is that these desires lack requisite cognitive equipment, being desires not informed by reasoned beliefs (of the type 'if I want *x*, I must do *y*'), beliefs which cannot be formed without language since beliefs have to be put in sentences we can assess in their truth or falsity; the desires of animals are thus rather more akin to feelings or sensations.[11] Another objection is that even if animals have needs, they still have no interests. Because to admit that animals have interests based on needs would require the admission that mere things, like cars, have interests; for taking a phrase like '*A* needs *x*' to mean that *x* is necessary for *A*'s survival or normal functioning, would be to reach the conclusion that just as a dog needs water to function or survive normally, so a tractor needs oil to function and a tree needs water to survive.[12] Against Singer, in particular, Frey makes the further point that his interest principle excludes interests in the case of persons whose capacity for pain is muted or entirely absent; a person, for example, can have interests even if totally unconscious or totally unable, owing to spinal and neurological injuries, to experience pain.[13]

Frey's objections, too, do not seem really tenable, outflanked as they are by other arguments. For one thing, Frey requires a degree of cognitive equipment which even children, especially those just born or unborn, cannot satisfy. For another, it is surely possible to admit that animals have interests, especially where we recognise that to say that a being, human or animal, needs kindness, is to say that it suffers or is hurt by our neglect or brutality. It is this dimension of feeling and need that children and animals share, not to be sure to the same extent, but still sufficiently to be able to distinguish their needs from the more functional needs of tractors or trees. Again, though it is true that an interest cannot require actual physical pain, such as where a person is neurologically incapable of feeling pain, this cannot possibly mean that physical pain is always unnecessary, or even untypical, for the creation of an interest, for if this were so the word interest would in fact become redundant in all situations of physical injury.

These comments are not at all meant to suggest that animals and (especially young) children, as they have similar interests, therefore qualify for similar rights. It is still necessary to differentiate between the two since we can say of a child what we can never say of an animal, namely, that the former is a potential right-holder who, in the natural and normal course of events, will become an actual one, so much so that he can, when the time comes, personally make claims or present grievances even about earlier injuries or past neglects. An animal, on the other hand, never evolves to that point. Lacking comparable cognitive equipment, language in particular, an animal is never able to formulate its interests or to make claims; hence it belongs to a category of beings who always and inevitably require a human custodian or representative to interpret or claim its particular needs or interests. The fact remains that even if we deny it rights we are yet able to say, echoing but not really following Feinberg or Singer, that an animal can have interests. For unless we allow an animal an interest against suffering, or an interest in human kindness, it is difficult to see how human beings could be required not to be cruel to it. This is so even where we proscribe cruelty on classical Bentham–utilitarian principles which take the infliction of pain to be a wrong, for the simple reason that harm or pain implies suffering by each object of our cruelty.

Let it be noted that to justify a rule or law against cruelty is not the same as enacting laws for the protection of our material or cultural heritage. The difference is that in the case of an animal we wish to protect it against torment, to prevent its suffering, quite apart from assuaging our own human sympathies. As regards our cultural heritage, however, our efforts at preservation only serve our own hopes or aspirations, usually depending on the sort of cultural or aesthetic ideals we entertain from time to time. Nor does a rule against cruelty commit itself to an animal's right to life *per se*, its purpose is only to prevent the infliction of pain. The point of this is that a rule against cruelty does not commit us to become vegetarians if the killing of animals can be achieved absolutely painlessly. Perhaps a utilitarian would not even wish to press his vegetarian views if this produced, everything considered, undesirable consequences for mankind: if (for example) a vegetarian world were subjected to a protein deficiency detrimental to health.

INTERESTS, CLAIMS, COMMUNITY: FINAL REMARKS

Again we see how misleading the notion of interest can be in relation to rights, to what constitutes a right especially. We certainly need an interest if only to ensure we do not make claims about matters in which we have no concern whatever; for we cannot have individual rights, as we argued in an earlier chapter, unless we can show that the right we are claiming contains something of a personal benefit to the claimant. Still, to have a personal interest or benefit in something is far from the end of it. I may be interested in music or early morning walks, this being entirely my affair as I can do what I like if there is nothing to stop me; claims and rights have nothing to do with any such interested activities. Claims in fact only arise when my interest is not descriptive – as the interests just mentioned – but is normative, hence is an interest which is to avail against another person, or many other persons, which person or persons, moreover, will have to respond to, or be answerable, to my claims, for, as we also tried to explain at earlier points, only answerable claims can qualify as rights *vis-à-vis* another.

What is more, claims cannot become answerable unless the individuals making or defending claims against each other make up a community which settles its adversarial disputes not by allowing those physically or psychologically more dominant simply to control those less so, but a community which manages its disputes discursively, that is, on the basis of certain rights which can only be moral rights. For only within such a discursive and moral community, one consisting of free and equal individuals, free and equal now understood in a broadly negative sense, can rights be at all had or claimed. Also, as rights-talk now becomes possible, it presupposes, precisely because of its being the talk it is, some basic individual rights, the rights to life, limb and property in particular: rights which indeed we can call natural rights since they must 'naturally' or necessarily be there if there is to be a community of free and equal, as well as rights-talking, individuals to begin with.

In practice, no doubt, our daily concern is not with these basic natural rights, but rather with the many and more prominent positive rights, that is to say positive rights (*in rem*) against everybody or positive rights (*in personam*) against particulars – positive so-called because they specifically define rights with regard to their actual enforceabilities. The fact remains that such positive rights, too, still presume that there be a moral community with prior (natural) rights, rights which give an individual claims against interference by another as well as rights which accord him an opportunity to exercise his own will over a *res*, so as to create a right of property; for unless he has these rights he would not be free to pursue his activities, nor be able to make transactions, whether by contract or gift or mere permissions, in respect of things or other assets or advantages. In the end we therefore have to go back to natural rights if we want to understand the nature also of positive rights as rights – as rights not imposed from above but functioning as a sort of moral currency between individuals.

Notes and References

1 RIGHTS, CLAIMS AND ENTITLEMENTS

1. The words 'propositional' and 'performative' come from J. Feinberg, 'The Nature and Value of Rights', *Journal of Value Inquiry*, 4 (1970) pp. 243, 252, 257; *Social Philosophy* (New Jersey, 1973) p. 65.
2. Alan R. White, 'Rights and Claims', *Law and Philosophy*, 1 (1982) p. 315; see on this also N. D. MacCormick, 'Rights, Claims and Remedies', p. 337, and White's reply,.p. 359, all in the same issue.
3. White, 'Rights and Claims', pp. 329–330, p. 331.
4. Ibid., p. 329.
5. H. J. McCloskey, 'Rights', *Philosophical Quarterly*, 15 (1965) pp. 115–127; 'Rights – Some Conceptual Issues', *Australasian Journal of Philosophy*, 54 (1976) pp. 99–115; see also R. A. Wasserstrom, 'Rights, Human Rights and Racial Discrimination', *Journal of Philosophy*, 61 (1964) pp. 628, 630.
6. McCloskey, 'Rights', p. 118; 'Rights – Some Conceptual Issues,' p. 100.
7. Feinberg, 'Nature and Value of Rights', p. 256.
8. McCloskey, 'Rights – Some Conceptual Issues', p. 104.
9. Ibid., p. 103.
10. The notion of 'subjunctive' claims is taken from White, 'Rights and Claims', p. 318 and *passim*. White distinguishes between 'indicative', 'subjunctive' and 'possessive' claims. The first assert that something *is* such and such, the second that something *be* so and so, while possessive are those claims, of the first or second kind, one already has. White admits that this distinction does not always make it clear whether a particular claim is indicative or subjunctive, although it must be one of the two. Even a legal claim can be a claim that one should have a remedy, or an indicative claim that one is already entitled to one. The distinction, however, is useful as it does separate the different types of grounds or reasons supporting claims.
11. J. Feinberg, 'Duties, Rights and Claims', *American Philosophical Quarterly*, 3 (1966) pp. 137, 142.
12. Ibid., pp. 152–4; Feinberg, *Social Philosophy*, p. 67.

2 RIGHTS AS DEFENCES AND LIBERTIES

1. In the limited sense in which English law allows such a right, i.e. the right of trying to persuade people to stop and listen, not of actually stopping

them for however short a time; see *Broome* v. *D.P.P.* [1974] A.C. 587.
2. See R. W. Downie, 'The Right to Criticise', *Philosophy*, 44 (1969) p. 116.
3. D. D. Raphael, 'Human Rights', *Aristotelian Society Supplement*, 39 (1965) pp. 206–7; and see also his *Problems of Political Philosophy* (London, 1970) pp. 68–70.
4. Raphael, 'Human Rights', pp. 210–11. The rights to work and to seek asylum now form part of the United Nations' Universal Declaration of Human Rights.
5. Ibid., p. 208.
6. See G. Marshall, 'Rights, Options and Entitlements', in A. W. B. Simpson (ed.) *Oxford Essays in Jurisprudence* (1973) pp. 228, 231–2.
7. Glanville Williams, 'The Concept of Liberty', in R. S. Summers (ed.) *Essays in Legal Philosophy* (Oxford, 1968) pp. 121, 136ff.
8. Ibid., p. 144.
9. Ibid., p. 141.
10. Williams also refers (ibid., p. 145) to the 'liberty' of the gaoler to keep the convict imprisoned, a liberty which is protected since the convict is now under a duty to submit. Such liberties, however, are much better considered as 'powers', powers belonging to certain offices which we discuss in Chapter 6.
11. H. L. A. Hart, 'Bentham on Legal Rights', in A. W. B. Simpson (ed.) *Oxford Essays in Jurisprudence*, pp. 171–201, 174ff.
12. Ibid., p. 180.
13. Ibid.

3 RIGHTS, BENEFITS AND INTERESTS

1. See D. Lyons, 'Rights, Claimants and Beneficiaries', *American Philosophical Quarterly*, 6 (1969) pp. 173, 176; D. N. MacCormick, 'Rights in Legislation', in Hacker and Raz (eds) *Law, Morality and Society* (Oxford, 1977) pp. 189, 204ff.
2. H. L. A. Hart, 'Bentham', *Proceedings of the British Academy*, 48 (1962), pp. 297, 314–5; 'Are There any Natural Rights', *Philosophical Review*, 64 (1955) pp. 175, 180–2; 'Bentham on Legal Rights', in A. W. B. Simpson (ed.) *Oxford Essays in Jurisprudence* (Oxford, 1973) p. 171.
3. One may also question whether it is altogether correct to regard the criminal law as precluding the personal options allowed in civil law. A criminal victim, (say, the victim of an assault) may choose not to prosecute or bring charges against the offender. At common law (disregarding modern legislation) such a person can technically 'waive' a crime. In the case of a felony he might be guilty of misprision of felony, that is, the offence of not disclosing a felony which to his knowledge has been committed. But this is a separate offence applying only to felonies, as well as being anyhow an offence against the community as a whole, the offence being precisely the waiving of the felony.
4. Hart, 'Are There any Natural Rights', pp. 180ff; 'Bentham on Legal Rights', pp. 195–6.
5. Hart, 'Bentham on Legal Rights', pp. 200–1.

6. Lyons, 'Rights, Claimants and Beneficiaries', p. 184; Hart, 'Are There any Natural Rights', p. 185.
7. In view of this and what he conceives as other difficulties (see 175ff), Lyons prefers to defend only what he calls a *qualified* benefit-theory. Not only, as above explained, does his last (and perhaps major) difficulty not really exist, his other qualifications, too, are better seen as comments on the notion of benefit itself, as this notion is ordinarily understood. Indeed, unless seen in a conventional light, a benefit-theory would yield results either incorrigibly absurd or too easily corrigible to be seriously entertained. Hence, assuming one agrees to adopt the latter rather than former alternative, we do not have to regard the theory as qualified, but can view it as the benefit-theory *tout court*. For a different criticism of Lyons, see T. R. Kearns, 'Rights, Benefits and Normative Systems', *Achiv für Rechts und Sozial Philosophie*, 61 (1975) p. 465, where the author tries to reaffirm the linkage of rights and benefits through what he calls an Adjustment Rules account of rights.
8. See on this J. Feinberg, *Social Philosophy* (New Jersey, 1973) p. 26; W. J. Rees, 'Public Interest', *Aristotelian Society Supplement*, 38 (1964) pp. 19ff; R. G. Frey, *Interests and Rights: The Case Against Animals* (Oxford, 1980) pp. 55, 78, 146.
9. Feinberg, *Social Philosophy*, p. 26.
10. See, in particular, Lamont, 'Rights', *Proceedings Aristotelian Society*, 24 (1950) p. 83; H. J. McCloskey, 'Rights', *Philosophical Quarterly*, 15 (1965) pp. 155, 166; D. N. McCormick, 'Right in Legislation', pp. 189, 192ff.

4 RIGHTS AND DUTIES

1. Bowring (ed.), Bentham, *Works*, iii (1843) pp. 159, 181.
2. See G. Marshall, 'Rights, Options and Entitlements', in A. W. B. Simpson (ed.) *Oxford Essays in Jurisprudence*, 2nd ser. (1973) pp. 228, 236–7.
3. Stuart M. Brown, Jr., 'Inalienable Rights', *Philosophical Review*, 64 (1955) pp. 192, 193–4.
4. M. G. Singer, *Generalisation in Ethics* (London, 1973) pp. 311, 315.
5. See R. B. Brandt, 'The Concept of Obligation and Duty', *Mind*, 73 (1964) pp. 374, 376.
6. 'Moral duties', Feinberg says, sounds odd in our ears: 'Duties, Rights, and Claims', *American Philosophical Quarterly*, 3 (1966) pp. 137, 140(n).
7. C. H. Whiteley, 'On Duties', *Proceedings Aristotelian Society*, 53 (1953) pp. 95, 97.
8. D. Lyons, 'The Correlativity of Rights and Duties', *Nous*, 4 (1970) pp. 45, 47ff.
9. For this example, see Lyons, ibid., pp. 54–5, who from his viewpoint also sees it differently.
10. See also D. Braybrooke, 'The Firm but Untidy Correlativity of Rights and Obligations', *Canadian Journal of Philosophy*, 1 (1972) pp. 351, 360–2.

11. M. G. Singer, 'The Basis of Rights and Duties', *Philosophical Studies*, 23 (1972) pp. 48, 49ff.
12. Singer, 'Rights and Duties', p. 49.
13. Ibid., pp. 52ff.
14. Braybrooke, 'Firm But Untidy Correlativity', p. 351.
15. C. Arnold, 'Analyses of Right', in E. Kamenka and A. S. Tay (eds) *Human Rights* (London, 1978) pp. 74, 77, 82ff.
16. See R. B. Brandt, *Ethical Theory* (New Jersey, 1959) p. 441.
17. W. D. Ross, *The Right and the Good* (Oxford, 1930) pp. 19ff, 28ff; *Foundations of Ethics* (Oxford, 1939) pp. 84ff. And see A. I. Melden, 'The Play of Rights', *Monist*, 56 (1972) pp. 479, 481ff., 491.
18. P. Jones, 'Doubts About Prima Facie Duties', *Philosophy*, 45 (1970) pp. 39, 43ff.
19. See e.g. B. A. Richards, 'Inalienable Rights: Recent Criticisms and Old Doctrine', *Philosophical and Phenomenological Research*, 29 (1969) pp. 391, 397.
20. On all this, see L. J. Russell, 'Ought Implies Can', *Proceedings Aristotelian Society*, 36 (1936) pp. 151, 181; Don Locke, 'Natural Powers and Human Abilities', *Proceedings Aristotelian Society* (1974) pp. 171, 177, 182, 185; R. M. Chisholm, 'The Descriptive Element in the Concept of Action', *Journal of Philosophy*, 61 (1964) pp. 613, 614ff.

5 A HOHFELDIAN DIGRESSION

1. Thomas D. Perry, 'A Paradigm of Philosophy: Hohfeld on Legal Rights', 14 (1977) *American Philosophical Quarterly*, p. 41.
2. Wesley N. Hohfeld, *Fundamental Legal Conceptions* (New Haven, 1964) pp. 35, 38ff.
3. M. Moritz, *Über Hohfelds System der Juridischen Grundbegriffe* (Lund, 1960) pp. 56, 58.
4. Hohfeld, *Fundamental Legal Conceptions*, pp. 36, 39.
5. *Quinn v. Leathem* [1901] A.C. 495; and see Hohfeld, *Legal Conceptions*, pp. 42ff; Perry, *A Paradigm of Philosophy*, pp. 44ff.
6. For similar such conflicting rights, see *Allen v. Flood* [1898] A.C.1.; *Mogul Steamship Co. v. McGregor [1892] A.C. 25; Sorrell v. Smith* [1925] A.C. 700; and *Crofter Hand Woven Harris Tweed Co. v. Veitch* [1942] A.C. 435.
7. Hohfeld, *Legal Conceptions*, p. 41.
8. Ibid., p. 42.
9. See, respectively, A. Kocourek, 'Non-Legal Content Relations', *Illinois Law Review* (1922) p. 233; 'The Hohfeld System', *Illinois Law Review*, 15 (1920) p. 24; J. Stone, *Legal System and Lawyers' Reasonings* (Sydney, 1964) pp. 139, 160; Pound *Jurisprudence*, vol. iv (1959) pp. 75ff. M. Moritz, *Uber Hohfelds System*, pp. 72ff, 85. For some defence of the no-right, see, however, P. Mullock, 'The Hohfeldian No-Right', *Archiv f. Rechts und Sozial-Philosophie*, 56 (1970) p. 265.
10. Hohfeld, *Fundamental Legal Conceptions*, p. 48note.

11. Ibid., p. 39.
12. Fred B. Fitch, 'A Revision of Hohfeld's Theory of Legal Concepts', *Logique et Analyse*, 10 (1967) pp. 269, 270.
13. Ibid., p. 272.
14. Hohfeld, *Fundamental Legal Conceptions*, pp. 50–1.
15. Ibid., p. 60note.
16. See Moritz, *Über Hohfelds System*, pp. 101ff.
17. Hohfeld, *Fundamental Legal Conceptions*, pp. 51ff, 58–9.

6 PERMISSION, POWER AND PRIVILEGE

1. See on this G. H. von Wright, *Norm and Action* (London, 1963) p. 87; J. Raz, *Practical Reason and Norms* (London 1975) pp. 85ff.
2. H. von Wright, *Norm and Achion*, p. 90.
3. *Thomas v. Sorrell* (1973) Vaugh. 330, 351.
4. If the original transaction happens to be gratuitous, or ambiguous, or voidable on any ground, the grant will fail in law, and the permission be construed as revocable: see e.g. *Wood v. Leadbitter* (1845) 13 M. & W. 838; *Goldsack v. Shore* [1950] 1 K.B. 708.
5. H. L. A. Hart, *The Concept of Law* (Oxford, 1961) pp. 27–8, 42–3; J. Raz, *Practical Reason* pp. 98–104.
6. For the historical association of right with power, see J. Finnis, *Natural Law and Natural Rights* (Oxford, 1979) pp. 206ff.
7. H. L. A. Hart, 'Bentham on Legal Powers', *Yale Law Journal*, 81 (1972) pp. 799, 803–5.
8. Bentham *Of Laws in General* (London, 1970), p. 256.
9. The view of powers here advanced receives a passing mention in Bentham, pp. 270–1, when he discusses such powers as the trust which have 'a command super-added to it', the trustee being under a duty to do something for another's benefit. But for Bentham such powers belong to a special ('fiduciary') category; they are not at all his prototype of powers, his principal type rather being those powers, earlier referred to, which are 'exclusive' and 'exceptional': see pp. 27, 56–7, 255–7. Hart, too, refers to something similar when discussing what he calls 'unilateral liberties': 'Bentham on Legal Rights', p. 182. Unilateral liberties are described as rights to do actions together with duties, some individuals being not merely permitted but required to do some act generally prohibited, Hart giving the example of the policeman who when asked what right he has cites his orders. Even so, the connection of unilateral liberties with powers is left very unclear: Hart, p. 196; and, in any case, his main argument concerning powers does not rest on unilateral but on bilateral liberties. Hart's whole discussion seeks to make the power (together with attendant notions of choice and control) the centre of all rights – the ordinary right correlative to duty being for him 'only a special case of legal power in which the right-holder is at liberty to waive [etc.] another's obligations': p. 197. If the analysis presented in the text is even approximately correct,

Hart's views seem to be putting matters quite the wrong way round.

10. See generally A. R. White, 'Privilege', *Modern Law Review*, 41 (1978) p. 299, to which the present discussion owes a good deal.
11. Ibid., p. 302.
12. Ibid., p. 306.
13. Hart, 'Bentham on Legal Rights', pp. 198–9.
14. See also J. Raz, 'Professor Dworkin's Theory of Rights', *Political Studies*, 26 (1978) pp. 123, 125n.
15. Hohfeld, *Fundamental Legal Conceptions* (New Haven, 1964) pp. 50, 60–3; and see Chapter 5.
16. For a totally different view, see however C. Wellman, 'A New Conception of Human Rights', in Kamenka and Tay (eds), *Human Rights* (London, 1978) pp. 48–58.
17. Bentham, *Of Laws in General*, pp. 200–1.
18. For a good account, see D. G. Ritchie, *Natural Rights* (London, 1952) pp. 244ff.

7 FROM POSITIVE TO NATURAL RIGHTS

1. Feinberg, *Social Philosophy* (New Jersey, 1973) p. 67.
2. B. Bandman, 'The Notion of Human Rights', *American Philosophical Quarterly*, 6 (1969) pp. 240, 246; R. Wasserstrom, 'Rights, Human Rights and Racial Discrimination', *Journal of Philosophy*, 61 (1964) pp. 628, 630, 636; A. I. Melden, 'The Play of Rights', *Monist*, 56 (1972) pp. 479, 499.
3. R. Young, 'Dispensing with Moral Rights' *Political Studies*, 6 (1978) pp. 63, 67–8.
4. For another view, see R. M. Dworkin, *Taking Rights Seriously* (London, 1977) pp. 81ff, and by the same author 'No Right Answer', in P. M. S. Hacker and J. Raz (eds), *Law, Morality and Society* (Oxford, 1977) pp. 58, 78.
5. Stuart M. Brown, 'Inalienable Rights', *Philosophical Review*, 64 (1955) pp. 92, 195. See also M. P. Golding, 'Towards a Theory of Human Rights', *Monist*, 52 (1968) pp. 521, 529, 532ff.
6. M. MacDonald, 'Natural Rights', *Proceedings Aristotelian Society*, 47 (1947) pp. 225, 238–9.
7. W. K. Frankena in R. B. Brandt (ed.) *Social Justice* (New Jersey, 1962) pp. 5ff.
8. J. S. Mill, *Utilitarianism*, chapter 5, par. 15.
9. Ibid., paras 24–25.
10. See on this D. Lyons, 'Human Rights and the General Welfare', *Philosophy and Public Affairs*, 6 (1977) pp. 113, 125–6.
11. G. Vlastos, 'Justice and Equality', in R. B. Brandt (ed.), *Social Justice* (New Jersey, 1962) pp. 21, 43ff. Another theory, despite other differences, similarly holds equality to rest in the end on our taking 'a human point of view' that accords full respect to a person as such irrespective of his occupation, position or title: B. Williams, 'The Idea of

Equality', in *Problems of the Self* (Cambridge, 1973) pp. 230, 234ff.
12. See K. Nielsen, 'Scepticism and Human Rights', *Monist* 52 (1968) pp. 573, 580–1.
13. H. L. A. Hart, 'Are There Any Natural Rights?', *Philosophical Review*, 64 (1955) p. 175. Hart means this to be a 'conditional assertion', with the weight on the conditional 'if' ('if there are any moral rights'), though the point of this is to avoid 'ontological' commitments arising from the 'existence' of rights, this being therefore mainly a disclaimer made for cautionary purposes which does not affect the argument as a whole. Hart further insists that he is merely arguing for *one* natural right, not a series, but again this seems a minor point as he later speaks of 'general rights', all of them particular exemplifications of this one equal right to be free. A good deal of Hart's paper is taken up with arguments against the benefit-theory of rights, arguments we have already considered in Chapter 3.
14. Ibid., pp. 183–4, 188–90.
15. Ibid., p. 178.
16. Equality works out differently, certainly more positively, in the case of distribution – a matter we discuss in Chapter 9.
17. K. Baier, 'Reasons for Doing Something', *Journal of Philosophy*, 61 (1964) pp. 198, 200.
18. K. Britton, 'Concepts of Actions and Concepts of Approval', *Proceedings Aristotelian Society*, 73 (1973) pp. 105, 110, 113.
19. See J. Jarvis, 'Practical Reasoning', *Philosophical Quarterly*, 12 (1962) pp. 316, 317, 322–4. Jarvis even concludes (pp. 327–8) that there is no such distinctive reasoning as 'practical reasoning'; it is rather ordinary inductive or deductive reasoning which is inspired by one's choice ('I want *y*') and followed by action.
20. J. S. Mill, *Utilitarianism*, chapter 5.

8 LIFE, LIMB AND PROPERTY

1. For this view of rights, see the views mainly of Hart discussed in Chapter 3.
2. Under the rule that 'trespass is merged in a felony': cf. *Smith v. Selwyn* [1914] 3 K.B. 98.
3. See also Stuart M. Brown Jr., 'Inalienable Rights', *Philosophical Review*, 64 (1955) pp. 192, 205ff.
4. Glanville Williams, 'Consent and Public Policy', *Criminal Law Review* (1962) pp. 74, 154.
5. C. L. Ten, *Mill on Liberty* (Oxford, 1980) pp. 118–9.
6. See I. Berlin, 'Equality', *Proceedings Aristotelian Society*, 56 (1956) pp. 301, 309.
7. Marvin Schiller, 'Are There Any Inalienable Natural Rights', *Ethics*, 79 (1969) pp. 309, 313.
8. The classical examples are *Wilkes v. Wood* (1763) 19 St. Tr. 1153, and *Entick v. Carrington* (1765) 19 St. Tr. 1030.
9. *Ashby v. White* (1703) 2 Ld. Raym. 938, 950.
10. B. Williams, 'The Idea of Equality', in *Problems of the Self* (Cambridge, 1973) p. 238.

11. See Chapter 4.
12. See H. J. McCloskey, 'Rights – Some Conceptual Issues', *Australasian Journal of Philosophy*, 54(1976) pp. 99, 105ff.
13. McCloskey, 'Rights', pp. 107–8.
14. Stuart M. Brown, 'Inalienable Rights', pp. 206–7; Melden, 'The Play of Rights', *Monist*, 56 (1972) pp. 479, 480 and *passim*.
15. *Hume's Treatise of Human Nature*, ed. Selby-Bigge (Oxford, 1951) p. 505.
16. See, for example, Hume's appreciative comments on the merits of effort and labour in his *Enquiries*, ed. Selby-Bigge (Oxford 1955) 309n.
17. R. Wollheim, 'Equality and Equal Rights', *Proceedings Aristotelian Society*, 56 (1956) pp. 281, 282.
18. Ibid., p. 284.

9 RIGHTS TO WELFARE AND OTHER BENEFITS

1. Under the UN Universal Declaration of Human Rights, 1948. For a general discussion, see D. D. Raphael (ed.) *Political Theory and the Rights of Man* (1967) pp. 43ff, 101ff; E. Kamenka and A. E.-S. Tay (eds) *Human Rights* (London, 1978) pp. 1, 13, 113.
2. Hume, *Treatise of Human Nature* (Oxford, 1951) pp. 497, 531–2.
3. Ibid., pp. 484ff.
4. J. Raz, 'Principles of Equality', *Mind*, 87 (1978) pp. 321, 335–6.
5. R. Nozick, *Anarchy, State and Utopia* (Oxford, 1974) pp. 33, 169ff.
6. Laslett (ed.) *Two Treatises of Government* (Cambridge, 1970), p. 329.
7. Plato, *Laws*, 757a; Aristotle, *Nich. Ethics*, 1131a.
8. See T. Honderich, 'Principle of Equality', *Mind*, 90 (1981) pp. 481, 490, 495ff; and see also B. Williams, 'The Idea of Equality', in *Problems of the Self* (Cambridge, 1973) p. 248.
9. H. J. McCloskey, 'Human Needs, Rights and Political Values', *American Philosophical Quarterly* 13 (1976) pp. 1, 5ff. Several points hereafter owe a good deal to this article.
10. W. B. Gallie, 'Essentially Contested Concepts', *Proceedings Aristotelian Society*, 56 (1956), p. 167.
11. McCloskey, 'Human Needs, Rights and Political Values', pp. 7ff.
12. J. Rawls, *A Theory of Justice* (Oxford, 1972) pp. 17ff, 60ff.
13. McCloskey, 'Human Needs', p. 3 and *passim*.
14. Vlastos, 'Justice and Equality', in Brandt (ed.) *Social Justice* (New Jersey, 1962) pp. 63ff.

10 THE LIMITS OF RIGHTS

1. H. J. McCloskey, 'Rights – Some Conceptual Issues', *Australasian Journal of Philosophy*, 54 (1976) pp. 99, 113.
2. D. N. MacCormick, 'Children's Rights: A Test-Case for Theorists of Right', *Archiv für Rechts und Sozial Philosophie* 62 (1976) pp. 305, 307ff.
3. Ibid., pp. 309, 310–11, 312–13.

4. Ibid., p. 311.
5. Ibid.
6. J. Feinberg, 'The Right of Animals and Unborn Generations', in W. T. Blackstone (ed.) *Philosophy and Environmental Crisis* (University of Georgia Press, 1974) p. 61.
7. D. J. Ritchie, *Natural Rights* (London, 1952) pp. 107ff.
8. J. Feinberg, 'The Rights of Animals and Unborn Generations', pp. 43, 49ff.
9. P. Singer, *Animal Liberation* (London, 1976) pp. 8, 17; *Practical Ethics* (Cambridge, 1979) pp. 48ff.
10. *Animal Liberation*, pp. 9, 185; *Practical Ethics*, pp. 48ff, 50.
11. R. G. Frey, *Interests and Rights: The Case Against Animals* (Oxford, 1980) pp. 83, 88ff, 93ff.
12. Ibid., pp. 79, 82–3.
13. Ibid., pp. 145ff.

Index

alienable, inalienable rights, 28, 90
animals' rights, 27, 117, 122
Arnold, C., 47, 129
assertive rights, 13, 23, 65

Baier, K., 85, 132
Bandman, B., 74, 131
benefit theory, 27, 30, 127, 128
benefits and rights, 25, 28
Bentham, J., 36, 38, 67, 128, 130, 131
Berlin, I., 132
Brandt, R. B., 39, 128, 129
Braybrooke, D., 44, 128
Britton, K., 85, 132
Brown, Stuart M., Jr, 37, 78, 91, 128, 131, 133

charity as duty, 39, 40
children's rights, 117, 120
Chisholm, R. M., 50, 129
'choses' in action, 45
claims, and claiming, 1, 2, 4, 6, 10
  indicative, possessive claims, 126
  making claims, 4
  performative, propositional claims, 2, 4
  subjunctive claims, 10
claims and entitlements, 6
claim-rights, 23, 51
community and rights, 37, 92, 108, 120, 124
  communal model, 79, 120, 125
complementaries, rights, duties as 46, 49
conflicting rights, 53, 97
constitutional rights, 70, 93
contracts for third parties, 29
correlativity, rights, duties, 36, 44, 46
  and complementaries, 46
  degrees of, 44

defensive rights, 5, 13, 54
derivative, primary rights, 71, 72, 90
dichotomy of rights, 13, 22
disability, 42, 58, 61
discursive framework of rights, 84, 87
Downie, R. W., 14, 127
duties and rights, 36, 51
  duties in extended sense, 39
  'dutiless' rights, 9, 23, 40
duty–liberty relation, 56
duty-specificity, 47
Dworkin, R. M., 131

easements, right of way, 19, 65
Entick v. Carrington (1765), 132
entitlements as rights, 7
  and claims, 6
equality, freedom, and rights, 81, 83, 89, 113
exemptions, 57

Feinberg, J., 2, 7, 11, 32, 74, 121, 122, 126, 128, 131, 134
Finnis, J., 130
Fitch, F. B., 56, 130
Frankena, W. B., 80, 131
freedom, *see* equality
Frey, R. G. 123, 128, 134
future generations, rights of, 121

Gallie, W. B., 114, 133
generality of rights, 47

Hart, H. L. A., 20, 27, 29, 83, 127, 130, 132
Hohfeld, W. N., 23, 42, 51, 129
Honderich, T., 113, 133
human rights 105, 133
Hume, D., 101, 106, 133
'Hume's Law', 80, 87

immunities, 58, 61, 70
inalienable rights, 28, 90
incapacity and rights, 117, 120
indefeasible rights, 93
interest and right, 25, 31, 33, 34, 124
interest theory, principle, 31, 34, 117, 122

Jarvis, J., 87, 132
Jones, P., 49, 129
jural opposites, 51
justice and rights, 80, 89

Kocourek, A., 56, 129

Lamont, D., 128
legal rights, 74, 75, 97
liability, and power, 58
liberties, 13, 15, 18, 20, 22, 51, 56, 127
  and duties, 56
liberty-right, 51
  and privilege, 51, 68
liberty as political right, 94
life, limb, rights to, 90

McCloskey, H. J., 7, 9, 98, 114, 116, 126, 133
MacCormick, D. N., 118, 127, 133
MacDonald, M., 80, 131
Marshall, G., 30, 37, 127, 128
may and can, 5, 8, 17, 23, 36
Melden, A. I., 131, 133
Mill, J. S., 80, 89, 131, 132
Moritz, M., 51, 129
Mullock, P., 129

natural rights, 74, 77, 79, 83, 87, 95, 97, 125
  public natural rights, 93, 94
nature, as source of rights, 80
Nielsen, K., 132
no-rights, notion of, 52, 54
non-correlative duties, 38
non-correlative rights, 40
normative property, rights as, 27, 90
Nozick, R., 109, 133

obligations and duties, 39, 128
opposites, jural, 51
opposition, square of, 57
permissions, 63
Perry, T. D., 51, 129
positive rights 74, 97
Pound, R., 129
power, notion of, 41, 63, 65
  in Hohfeld, 51, 58
prima facie rights, duties, 11, 37, 48, 98
primacy of rights, 8, 47
primary, derivative rights, 71, 72
principles, moral, and rights, 75
privileges, 51, 63, 68
prohibition, 57
property, rights of, 90, 100, 102, 103
public natural rights, 93, 94

Quinn v. Leathem (1901), 52, 129

Raphael, D. D., 15, 127, 133
Rawls, J., 115, 133
Raz, J., 63, 66, 109, 130, 133
Richards, B. A., 49, 129
right-like notions 63
rights, conceptual elements, 2, 6, 12, 24, 36
  of animals, 27, 117, 122
  of children, 117
  and claims, 4
  defensive rights, 13
  derivative, primary rights, 71, 72
  and duties, 36
  and entitlements, 6
  in personam, in rem rights, 7, 33, 41, 44, 72
  of future generations, 121
  of incapacitated persons, 117, 120
  and interests, 31
  and liberties, 13
  manifesto rights, 11, 74
  and needs, 115, 116
  no rights, no rights, 36
  non-correlative rights, 40
  to self-defence, 13
  to vote, 28, 94
  see also natural, positive rights

Ritchie, D. J., 122, 131, 134

Ross, W. D., 48, 129
rules and rights, 36, 37

Schiller, M. 93, 132
self-defence, right to, 13
Singer, M. G., 42, 43, 129
Singer, P., 122, 134
Stone, J., 56, 129
subjunctive claims, 10

Ten, C. L., 92, 132

unequal rights, 71, 72
utility, utilitarianism, 81

Vlastos, G., 81, 116, 131, 133
volenti non fit injuria, 14, 22, 64, 92
vote, right to, 28, 94

waivable rights, 27, 90
Wasserstrom, R. A., 126, 131
welfare, rights to, 105
  quantum of, 112
Wellman, C., 131
White, A. R., 4, 6, 68, 69, 126, 131
Whiteley, C. H., 40, 128
will theory, 34
Williams, B., 45, 131, 132
Williams, Glanville, 18, 92, 127, 132
Wollheim, R., 102, 103, 133
Wright, G. H. von, 130

Young, R., 75, 131